REYNALDO HAHN

On Singers and Singing

Adelina Patti. Lithograph after a drawing by Pirodon, 1889. Bibliothèque de l'Opéra, Paris.

REYNALDO HAHN

On Singers and Singing
Lectures and an Essay

Translated by
Léopold Simoneau, O.C.

Introduction by Lorraine Gorrell
Discography by William R. Moran

Reinhard G. Pauly, General Editor

AMADEUS PRESS
Portland, Oregon

Cover: Reynaldo Hahn, composer-pianist-singer, March 1910.
Collection Roger-Viollet, Paris.

© Editions Gallimard, 1957, as *Du Chant,*
by Reynaldo Hahn.

Translation © 1990 by Amadeus Press
(an imprint of Timber Press, Inc.)
Discography © 1990 by William R. Moran Trust.
All rights reserved.

ISBN 0-931340-22-5
Printed in Hong Kong

AMADEUS PRESS
9999 S.W. Wilshire
Portland, Oregon 97225

Library of Congress Cataloging-in-Publication Data

Hahn, Reynaldo, 1875-1947.
    [Du chant. English]
    On singers and singing : lectures and an essay / Reynaldo Hahn ;
translated by Leopold Simoneau ; with an introduction by Lorraine
Gorrell ; Reinhard G. Pauly, general editor.
       p.   cm.
    Translation of: Du chant.
    A series of nine lectures Hahn gave 1913-14 plus an epilogue.
    ISBN 0-931340-22-5
    1. Singing--Instruction and study. 2. Music--Performance.
I. Title.
MT820.H1413   1989
783'.007--dc20   89-14987
                                                            CIP
                                                            MN

First published in Great Britain in 1990 by
Christopher Helm (Publishers) Ltd, Imperial House,
21-25 North Street, Bromley, Kent BR1 1SD

ISBN 0-7470-1420-5

Errata

We regret that two photographs in this volume are wrongly identified.

Page 22: Vanni Marcoux, French bass-baritone (1877–1962), in the title role of Mussorgsky's *Boris Godunov*.

Page 168: Pol Plançon, French bass (1854–1914), as St. Bris in Meyerbeer's *Les Huguenots*.

To

Madame ADOLPHE BRISSON,

in witness to my most respectful and grateful friendship.

R. H.

Fedor Chaliapin (*at right*) in the title role of Massenet's *Don Quichotte*. Courtesy Photo Archive of Benedikt & Salmon Record Rarities, San Diego.

CONTENTS

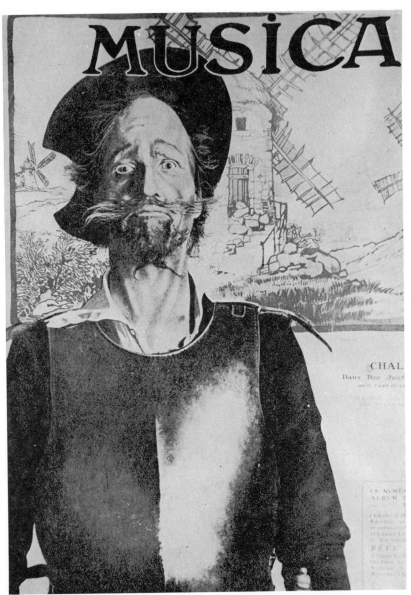

Fedor Chaliapin in Massenet's *Don Quichotte*. Cover of the review *Musica*, April 1910.

FOREWORD

Reynaldo Hahn's place in French music of the early 20th century is well described in the introduction by Lorraine Gorrell that follows. That many of Hahn's observations on the art of singing—on matters of style, taste and technique—are still quite relevant today was first pointed out to me by Richard Poppino, a fine singer and vocal pedagogue himself, quite at home in the French repertoire. As a student of Léopold Simoneau, he had become familiar with some of Hahn's writings which Mr. Simoneau was fond of quoting.

There was agreement that a translation of Hahn's remarks would be beneficial to English-speaking singers, for several reasons. The author offers much practical advice to aspiring singers, including remarks on effective communication with an audience. Actually, much of what Hahn says is also directed to these audiences, to the musically interested general public.

These chapters are far removed from being another "method on learning how to sing." Though they contain much information on vocal technique, they are also valuable to readers today for the picture they paint of Hahn's musical world: France (and Central Europe) during the first half of our century. Hahn's observations bring to life for us many of the great singers whom he heard, knew, accompanied and directed—singers who were internationally known for their interpretations of art song, opera and operetta. He finds words of praise for many but does not hesitate to express strong disapproval of individuals and their performances, and of the musical establishment in which they hoped to succeed, where commercial considerations too often took precendence over artistic standards, as they do today.

Our hope is that Hahn's broad musical knowledge, presented in a literary style that is typically French—often witty, sometimes sarcastic, occasionally a little long-winded—will make his observations informative and entertaining for all who love French song.

R. G. P.

PREFACE

This volume includes a series of nine lectures I gave in 1913 and 1914 at the *University of Annales*. The reader will therefore encounter a fairly informal style, some colloquial language and occasional repetition for review or emphasis. Some of this may be inappropriate in material conceived at the outset to be *read*. I trust the reader will find this approach excusable, keeping in mind the amount of improvisation that was necessarily a part of these lectures, and the casual demeanor that the speaker could allow himself before a young and friendly audience.

As a reminder of those circumstances, I decided to retain my references to the musical examples sung during these lectures [these are represented in the current edition by a line of asterisks] to illustrate various points I wished to make.

R. H.

Reynaldo Hahn, March 1910. Collection Roger-Viollet, Paris.

Reynaldo Hahn: Composer of Song, Mirror of an Era

by Lorraine Gorrell

"La voix! la voix humaine, c'est plus beau que tout!"[1]

Composer, conductor, singer, critic and author, Reynaldo Hahn (1874–1947) was a brilliant member of a brilliant artistic era in France. He was a classmate of Ravel, an intimate friend of Marcel Proust and Sarah Bernhardt, beloved student of Massenet, friend of Fauré and acquaintance of many other notables of his age, including Debussy, Stravinsky, Saint-Säens, Dyagilev and Nijinski. He is now remembered for only a few of his more than one hundred *mélodies,* but during his life he also achieved recognition and fame for his operas, operettas, concertos, quartets, ballet music and piano pieces. He was also one of the more powerful influences as director of the Paris Opéra, conductor at the Salzburg Festival and music critic for the newspaper *Figaro.* In spite of his fame in Europe, he is little known in the English-speaking world, where only a few of his songs appear in collections and a few reviews of his music and articles on his work have been published. He is perhaps most famous among French literary scholars, who know him because of his close relationship with the great writer Marcel Proust. Nevertheless, approximately seventy of his songs are still in print in France and "L'Heure exquise" is in the repertory of most singers of French song.

Like many other well-known French composers—César Franck, Gluck and Lully, to name a few—Reynaldo Hahn was not French by birth. Born in Venezuela on August 9, 1874,[2] to a Venezuelan-Catholic mother and a German-Jewish father, Hahn was the youngest of twelve children. The family moved to France when he was three years old. He is reputed to have made his "artistic *début*" at the age of six in the *salon* of the Princess Mathilde, cousin of Napoleon III:

> The child sang romantic excerpts from the comic operas of Offenbach [and] accompanied himself at the piano, holding his audience with charm and singing all the music which he had in his head.[3]

Hahn entered the Paris Conservatoire at the age of eleven, studying *solfège,* piano, harmony and composition. There, he demonstrated remarkable promise and fluency in composition. One of his classmates, Morpain, stated that if the composition class needed a manuscript for study, the teacher would

> turn towards our friend: "Reynaldo, write something for us." Reynaldo would place himself before a blank page and, ten minutes later, we would begin class.[4]

His earliest works were for voice and piano; *Si mes vers avaient des ailes, Rêverie* and *Mai* were all written by the time he was fifteen years old. His famous collection, *Chansons grises,* based on poems of Paul Verlaine and including the well-known "L'Heure exquise," was published in his eighteenth year, after his teacher, Jules Massenet, had introduced Hahn to the publisher, Heugel, who paid him 100 francs for the collection. Most of Hahn's songs were published by Heugel & Cie during his lifetime, and the majority of these songs appeared before 1912, although a few appeared as late as 1921. In spite of these initial successes, however, Hahn's career as a song-composer was over by 1921, for he had been gradually drawn into other areas of music such as opera, film music and operetta, where he found a larger audience for his compositions. His first opera, *L'Ile du rêve,* was performed at the Opéra-Comique in 1898 and was followed by a number of other successful operas, the last of which, *Le Oui des jeunes filles,* was produced after his death in 1949. Hahn's operetta *Ciboulette,* first produced in 1923 and still performed and recorded, was the highlight of his successful ventures into this genre.

Hahn's musical production was prodigious, yet he was also able to travel a great deal—to Italy, Russia, Germany, Austria and Egypt (a proposed trip to the U.S.A. never materialized)—and, like so many other musicians of the 19th and 20th centuries, he was a skilled writer. He carried on a voluminous correspondence with family and friends and was also a music critic for *Foeming* from 1908 to 1910, for the *Journal* from 1910 to 1914 and for *L'Excelsior* from 1919 to 1921; in 1933, he became music critic for *Le Figaro.* His other writings included *Du Chant* (1920) [translated in the present volume], *La Grande Sarah* (1930, about his friend Sarah Bernhardt), *Notes (Journal d'un musicien)* (1933), *L'Oreille au guet* (1937) and *Thèmes variés* (1946); and he collaborated with other writers in *Le Chanteur* (1931) and *L'Initiation à la musique.*

Hahn also acquired fame as a conductor. Not only did he conduct the season at Cannes, but he developed a reputation as a knowledgeable interpreter of Mozart's operas. In 1906, he was invited to conduct *Don Giovanni* in Salzburg with the great Lilli Lehmann as Donna Anna; he also conducted Mozart at the Opéra-Comique as well as at the Paris Opéra after 1945, when he became its director. Hahn devoted the first section of *Thèmes variés* to Mozart, with such subheadings as *"The Abduction from the Seraglio,"* "The Angel Mozart," "Mozart and Salzburg," "Variations on *Don*

Giovanni" and "On *The Marriage of Figaro.*" In his book *Notes (Journal d'un musicien)*, Hahn stated: "I am entirely taken by Mozart . . . *Don Giovanni, Le Nozze di Figaro, Così fan tutte*—there is my daily nourishment. This musical charm envelops and penetrates me."[5] . . .

Hahn's songs are distinctly French. They are restrained rather than dramatic or effusive, filled with subtle nuance and quiet statement, lyrical and not given to virtuosic display. Hahn was particularly sensitive to the inflections and rhythms of language and created songs in which text became the dominant element. In fact, words were a crucial element in Hahn's inspiration and response to composition and the arts in general. In a letter to his close friend, the concert pianist Edouard Risler, Hahn wrote:

> I am only moved in the theatre or when there are words! It is an inexplicable phenomenon, but certain. Before a purely instrumental work, I experience only admiration, but I am not involved. A musical phrase charms and delights me but it never moves me: it is only sentiment that moves me.[6]

Hahn's love of words can also be seen as a basis for his gift as a linguist, perhaps an inevitable talent in one whose mother spoke Spanish, whose father spoke German and who himself grew up speaking French. His song collection *Venezia* in Venetian dialect and his English song collection, *Love Without Wings,* are evidence of his talent. As an enlisted soldier in World War I, Hahn was a translator at the front.

Hahn devoted much of his creative life to the glorification of the singing voice and words: The majority of his works were songs, operas and operettas. He himself was also a singer and wrote much about singing, although he protested that he was not an "expert":

> I am not a singer, nor a teacher of singing. . . . I am a composer and have only a relative authority to speak on

an art so complex, so arduous, that even the specialists . . . are often contradictory.[7]

But he sang constantly. He was a well-known figure at some of the more distinguished European *salons,* performing either his own *mélodies* or those of other composers he admired. In a series of essays entitled *Thèmes variés,* he described a *soirée* in which he sang numerous songs by Fauré—*Lydia, Nell, Les Roses d'Ispahan, Soir, Le Secret* and *Le Parfum impérissable*—and was accompanied by Fauré himself. Hahn admired Fauré immensely and was proud of their friendship. In his *Thèmes variés* he quotes from a letter from Fauré: "It is infinitely agreeable to me to feel that, despite the difference in age, we are truly friends."[8]

One of Hahn's biographers, Bernard Gavoty, describes Hahn's singing:

I heard him [sing] only once, in Annales, too little to speak of him at length, enough to be entranced. Was it beautiful? No, it was unforgettable. The voice was nothing exceptional . . . a fine baritone voice, not very large, flexible as grass, ruled with a marvellous intelligence, a reflective divination. An interminable cigarette dangled from the line of his lips, not as a "pose" but out of habit. He sang as we breathe, out of necessity.[9]

Similar words are used to describe the Marquis de Poitiers, a character whom Marcel Proust, in his posthumously published novel, *Jean Santeuil,* presumably patterned after Hahn:

He had a charming voice and kept his cigarette in the corner of his mouth all the time he was singing, while his head moved with a sort of nervous twitch, though normally he was a somewhat lymphatic young man. Every word of the songs and musical-comedy numbers with which he entertained them, was clearly audible. He went on endlessly, stressing the rhythm of the accompaniment, singing the woman's part—in the case of a duet—in a light head-voice [falsetto], and thundering out the choruses.[10]

Hahn's repertoire included songs in a variety of languages, and his performances were noted for their expressiveness, precision of articulation and nuance without any trace of mannerism.[11]

Despite his claim that he was not a singer, Hahn had much to say about singers and singing. During the years 1913 and 1914, he gave two series of lectures on singing at the University of Annales that were later compiled into a book, *Du Chant* (1920), reissued in 1957 by Gallimard [and again, in English translation, in 1989 in the present volume]. . . .

Hahn probably wrote many of his songs for his own voice and temperament—a temperament that was comfortable in the elegant world of the *salon*. He was described by one of Proust's biographers, William Sansom, as "pale brown, handsome, gifted, Jewish, moustached";[12] "at Mme Lemaire's, he played and sang his compositions to great applause and became a star of the *salon*."[13] The *salons* represented an important artistic meeting-place for the intellectual community in Paris and provided an intimate setting in which the composers of chamber music and song could find a sympathetic, sophisticated audience. A similar setting in early 19th-century Germany provided a background for the flowering of the *Lied*, although the *Lied* flourished among the cultivated German *bourgeoisie*, while in France it was typically the aristocracy who provided the setting for the developing *mélodie*. Many of Fauré's songs, for example, were first performed privately at the home of Princesse de Polignac, where the *avant-garde* of France, including Stravinsky, Manuel de Falla, Satie and Chabrier, met.[14] Ravel, Debussy, Anatole France, Proust and many other noted artists, at one time or another in their artistic lives, enjoyed the aristocratic and artistic society of the *salons* and realized that this was one of the few outlets for performance of intimate musical works. Romain Rolland declared that "in France, art has always had an aristocratic character. . . . The Republic still continued to regard music as something outside the people."[15] He pointed out that musical development within France was hindered because of a dearth of concert halls in Paris:

> In spite of the progress of music and musical taste, Paris has not yet a concert hall, as the smallest provincial towns in Germany have; and this shameful indifference, unworthy of the artistic renown of Paris, obliges the symphonic societies to take refuge in circuses or theatres, which they share with other kinds of performers, though the acoustics of these places are not intended for concerts.[16]

The *salons* provided a place where musicians could have their music heard by a sophisticated audience. Hahn discussed the world of the *salon* and its importance in the development of the *mélodie* in *Thèmes variés:*

> The most beautiful "mélodies" [were written] for the limited, chosen audience, for the cultivated minds . . . members of this society, in divers degrees . . . , perceive the thought, the intention, the talent of the poet and the musician. . . . But the *mélodie* for voice and piano, the *Lied,* as it has been called, is essentially *musique de chambre,* that is to say, of the *salon.* It is to be sung in the *salons* . . . intimate assemblies like those for whom Beethoven wrote *An die ferne Geliebte* and the touching *Adelaide.* It is for the *salons* that Schubert composed not only *Die schöne Müllerin* and *Winterreise* but also *Erlkönig* and *Doppelgänger.* It is there, in a little circle of attentive and acute minds, that they produce their total effect and where they exercise, with all their desired force, their mystical action.[17]

Hahn, a highly intelligent, cultured man, frequented many of the fashionable *salons* of his day, and it was at the home of the artist

Madeleine Lemaire that he, at the age of 19, met his lifelong friend Marcel Proust in 1894. Many aspects of Hahn's life, character and interests are revealed in the published letters of Proust. Their relationship began as a passionate love affair and grew into an enduring friendship that lasted until Proust's death in 1922. Proust was devoted to Hahn and, in a letter to Hahn's cousin Marie Nordlinger, Proust wrote: "Thanks to Reynaldo (everything I have ever done is thanks to Reynaldo), I met Whistler one evening.[18] He was sensitive to the criticisms, encouragements and judgments of Hahn and "took Reynaldo's slightest reservations about his writing extremely seriously."[19] He used Hahn as the model for the character mentioned earlier, the Marquis de Poitiers in his novel *Jean Santeuil,* and also represented Hahn in another character, Henri de Réveillon (initials are the reverse of R. H.), best friend of the novel's main character; the name Henri de Réveillon also recalls the *château* Réveillon where Hahn and Proust stayed in the early days of their romance. . . .

Hahn played a conservative role in the formation of the French art song. He obviously shunned the complex harmonic directions in which Debussy was leading and did not show the technical variety and originality of Fauré. Yet his careful setting of poetry, the uncluttered simplicity of his accompaniments and the modest range of dynamics and pitch contribute toward the creation of songs whose charms will reveal themselves only to the performer who is sensitive to the text and its meaning. Hahn, a singer of great refinement, was able to present his songs to the public with subtlety and finesse; these characteristics are also required of the modern singer, as an early critic noted:

> A great deal of success of these songs depends upon interpretation. The sympathetic hand and tender voice must be brought to bear upon them . . . you can realize what the composer is able to accomplish only when you hear his compositions performed by a sympathetic exponent.[20]

This essay, in expanded form, first appeared in *The Music Review,* Vol. 46, No. 4 (November, 1985). It is reprinted here with the permission of the author and publisher.

[1]Reynaldo Hahn, in a letter to Edouard Risler (quoted in Bernard Gavoty, *Reynaldo Hahn: Le musicien de la belle époque* (Paris, 1976), p. 186).

[2]Although Hahn's military records list his year of birth as 1875, his birth certificate and baptismal records are dated 9th August, 1874, according to Daniel Bendahan, *Reynaldo Hahn: Su vida y su obra* (Caracas, 1973), p. 13.

[3]Gavoty, *op. cit.,* pp. 26–27.

[4]*Ibid.,* p. 37.

[5]Reynaldo Hahn, *Notes (Journal d'un musicien)* (Paris, 1933), p. 134.

[6]Gavoty, *op. cit.,* p. 60.

[7]Reynaldo Hahn, *Du Chant* (Paris, 1920), p. 13.

[8]Reynaldo Hahn, *Thèmes variés* (Paris, 1946), p. 137.

[9]Gavoty, *op. cit.,* p. 193.

[10]Marcel Proust, *Jean Santeuil,* trans. Gerard Hopkins (New York, 1956), pp. 455–456.

[11]In his *Notes (Journal d'un musicien),* p. 4, Hahn recounts the comments of the famous singer Pauline Viardot and her statements on the naturalness of his singing.

[12]Willam Sansom, *Proust and His World* (New York, 1973), p. 5.

[13]J. E. Rivers, *Proust and the Art of Love* (New York, 1980), p. 66.

[14]Robert Orledge, *Gabriel Fauré* (London, 1979), p. 18.

[15]Romain Rolland, *Musicians of Today,* trans. Mary Blaiklock (New York, 1969), p. 18.

[16]*Ibid.,* p. 281.

[17]Hahn, *Thèmes variés,* pp. 180–181.

[18]Marcel Proust, *Letters of Marcel Proust,* edited by Mina Curtiss (New York, 1949), p. 93.

[19]Rivers, *op. cit.,* p. 71.

[20]D. C. Parker, "The Songs of Reynaldo Hahn," *The Musical Standard,* Vol. VIII, No. 208 (London, 1916), p. 453.

Pol Plançon, French bass (1854–1914), as St. Bris in Meyerbeer's *Les Huguenots.*
Courtesy Photo Archive of Benedikt & Salmon Record Rarities, San Diego.

I

Why Do We Sing?

Mesdames, Mesdemoiselles, Messieurs,

Upon seeing the announcement of these lectures on the art of singing, many people must have questioned my motives. I am not a singer, nor a teacher of singing, nor a physiologist. I am a composer and have only relative authority to speak on an art so complex, so arduous, that even the specialists, after spending a lifetime in search of its secrets, are often contradictory. I am perfectly aware of the deficiency of my knowledge. I am quite overwhelmed to find myself before an audience which fills the hall. For a moment, I entertained the hope that these talks would take place in the intimacy of a small group of familiar faces in whose presence, without stage fright, without concern, I could chat as I do when I am with friends. I could have engaged in a sort of mental meandering, without a set plan, sitting at the piano now and then to illustrate with examples what I am propounding. Indeed it was at the conclusion of just such a wandering conversation, during which we discussed many issues related to singing, that Mme Brisson asked me to come here to repeat some of those remarks to you. She insisted in such a charming, friendly yet firm way that I at last accepted.

So here I am, ready to take up arms against bad singers and incompetent teachers whose crimes I confess I may exaggerate. But I will not conceal the fact that in spite of my grand preparations for battle, I tremble more than a little. For I see here before me an imposing audience; some are unknown faces, some are very serious, and some are even more intimidating because they smile. And I am afraid that those faces will say: "But, who are you to come here and criticize singers and those who teach singers? Do you think that it is enough to murmur a few *mélodies*, with half-closed lips, in a room barely eight meters square, and then go on to criticize honest and experienced people who know a great deal more about the subject than you?"

Believe me, during the few hours that we shall spend together, I shall avoid stating in a superior, all-knowing way even those things of which I am absolutely certain. I have too often observed the ephemeral nature of the most deeply held personal convictions in matters of singing and the fragility of the most rigorous reasoning to believe that I can invoke the former in my favor or that I can convince you of my own view by the latter. What I say will be said in the firm belief that I may be wrong and that I may well change my views on some or all of these matters one day.

Moreover, I shall rely much more on instinct than on my limited knowledge of singing; these remarks will turn on some quite subjective ideas and will therefore very likely be warmly disputed. I must also warn you that I will in all probability sing from time to time in order to be better understood, to make a certain point. I want to assure you that I do not presume to be an accomplished singer. When I criticize what I think is bad and then sing, do not think that I imagine my singing to be good. Simply view my modest demonstrations as sketchy, rough examples offered by someone who is not a professional singer, someone who has never trained his voice and who, on the contrary, is destroying what little voice he once had by smoking constantly, staying up too late, talking too much, and generally ignoring all rules of vocal hygiene.

So, to repeat, I shall not pretend to show you how the singer should proceed, but only suggest the approximate result which should be sought. Furthermore, if I were called upon to outline a rigorous singing method, I would find myself in an embarrassing situation, since I have always sung by instinct, and consequently my limited stock of technical ideas have resulted from analyzing what I have done after the fact and then comparing the outcome with what others have done. I have also been a keen observer of whatever is related to singing, from the sobbing of a child or the shrill cries of a street merchant to the brilliant vowels in the words of the police officer commanding the traffic to "move along" or the modulations in the voice of a deputy struggling to find the right words as he stands before the National Assembly.

Indeed, Mesdemoiselles, for someone who is deeply interested in singing, nothing in the domain of vocal sound or sound vibrations in general is useless: The briefest utterance, the least sound, the slightest noise, contains some kind of lesson; and one of the most severe charges that I bring against singers is that they are not curious about everything that concerns their art, that they make no effort to glean information from every corner. I have had the privilege of spending a good deal of time with the young but already renowned composer Stravinsky, who possesses a prodigious talent for orchestration. Just as Théophile Gautier used to say: "I am a man for whom the exterior world exists," so M. Stravinsky could say: "I am a man for whom the world of sound exists." The slightest resonance or vibration arouses his attention: a fork striking a glass, a cane lightly touching a chair, the rustle of a silken cloth, the grating of a door, the sound of footsteps. His infallible ear is immediately alert and prompt to analyze these sounds for new musical ideas. I wish singers would evince the same interest, but I shall not experience that pleasure soon because most of them, far from being interested in these modest events of everyday life, are scarcely concerned even with the voice and singing itself. Their colleagues are conceived only as competitors; they could not care less about those many first-rate singers they could listen to with profit virtually everywhere: in churches, theaters, music halls (where one sometimes encounters remarkable singers). For most, their art is but a means of realizing success, a way of satisfying their egos and securing material rewards. I shall frequently return to this theme of the singer's outlook and its possible provenance.

I myself simply do not understand this point of view. I have loved singing from the bottom of my heart since my earliest years, and it is this love alone that gives me the right to appear before you to speak about singing. True love gives rise to profound insights; and so, in matters of singing, I am convinced that I have understood things I have not specifically learned but somehow divined due to the depth of my love.

However, as you will readily understand, knowledge acquired in this manner may lack the solid basis and method necessary to suggest to me a logical order or a wisely mapped-out strategy of presentation. So please permit me to elaborate gradually on the topics I have chosen to address in this lecture, speaking as thoughts and recollections occur to me, mixing quotations and anecdotes into explanations of the vocal mechanism, or technical details into short analyses of particular expressive sounds. Not only will this casual approach give our meetings a more relaxed, less didactic quality, but also, I believe it to be most appropriate to the art of singing. And here we are at the heart of our subject.

Indeed (I shall repeatedly return to this refrain in the hope that I may finally convince you), what constitutes the real beauty and value, the final *raison d'être,* of singing, is the combination, the mixing, the indissoluble union of sound and thought. No matter how beautiful a sound may be, it is nothing if it expresses nothing. To admit that we are partial to the purely sensuous beauty of a voice is to confess to a certain weakness or susceptibility to the physical. Conversely, to find pleasure in a singer whose articulation and delivery are skilled but who lacks true singing ability is to prove that we care very little for music but prefer mere declamation.

The secret of singing is difficult to define: It lies in a close association of the speaking and the singing voice. Naturally, a beautiful sound is very appealing; there is unquestionably a great beauty in the fullness, softness, richness, flexibility and range of an exceptional voice. The Italians of old attached so much importance to this aspect of singing that they often neglected the other elements essential to the art (we shall address this matter in greater detail when we discuss *bel canto* a bit later). Indeed, a beautiful voice controlled by the will of the singer, whether naturally beautiful or made so by training, is a most beautiful thing even in the absence of the intellectual element that should be added to it. However, a beautiful voice does not suffice; it may produce a pleasant sensation, but this has nothing to do with the real beauty of singing.

Let me repeat: The genuine beauty of singing consists in a perfect union, an amalgam, a mysterious alloy of the singing and the speaking voice, or, to put it better, the melody and the spoken word.

In singing, melody represents the spiritual element that gives the words an additional intensity, force, subtlety, poetry, charm or exoticism in ways that elude analysis but through which we experience enchantment without being able to say why. The spoken word, on the contrary, laden with sentiment and thought, gives melody a heightened significance, gives it the power to precisely and immediately affect our minds and hearts. If, between the spoken word and the melody, one had to dominate, there is no doubt that it ought to be the word; common sense commands it, as does artistic sense. If Victor Cousin could state categorically: "The great law of the arts is expression," how then could expression not be the supreme law of an art whose means of communication are speech and song? Or to repeat Wagner's apostrophe to music: "We have created you to be so beautiful only to subdue you; you shall never be, you should never be other than the spouse; and the word, your eternal lord, will reign eternally over you."[1]

So you see, there is no question here of an equal collaboration, but rather of the submission of music to the word. Diderot had already formulated this idea when he wrote: "One must consider lyric declamation like a line and singing like a second line that crisscrosses the first one; and the more this declamation, itself a type of singing, is interlaced with the singing line, touching at many points, the more genuine, the more beautiful the singing itself will be."[2]

My mind was full of these ideas when, barely an adolescent and a student of piano and harmony at the Conservatoire, I chanced to attend a series of vocal lessons. It seemed to me then that the teachers insisted almost exclusively on voice technique, on the purely vocal aspect of singing, and that they neglected and systematically overlooked what constitutes the psychological and imaginative aspect of this art. Whereupon I reacted, revolted, with the extreme excess of youth (I should say, of a child): I devoted all my attention to the other aspect of singing, that turning only on expression, on meaning. I set about singing in a way that, while perhaps not entirely lacking in interest, was unquestionably "anti-vocal."

This went on for many years. I was convinced that to sing well was to sing thus, in starts and stops, emphasizing realism, setting the words in stark relief, with no concern for tone production and control. And to me, those who proceeded otherwise, those for whom the voice and its control and care were a matter of constant concern, were "only singers." I used the term with disdain.

Well, I have changed my views. Obviously, I remain opposed to singing in which vocal virtuosity is the sole interest; I still will not admit that even the possessor of a beautiful and well-disciplined voice can ignore for any length of time the intellectual or emotional element. And, finally, I came to consider singing as not really a tangible thing, but malleable, in which sounds and words have equal importance, completing each other through some transcendent process of coordination, esthetic as well as mechanical, lending each other perpetual aid and collaborating in a joint action.

I will go further. I do not believe, in spite of many an opposing opinion, that one can "enunciate well" and sing altogether badly. Someone who sings well and enunciates badly does not interest me; if such singing is beautiful simply in itself, it would be infinitely better for that artist to limit himself to singing consecutive vowels without pronouncing words, but such singing could not be a work of art. The word, well articulated, well invested with thought, will place the voice naturally where it should be, will give it the color that it should have at each precise moment—and thus half the task is accomplished. As soon as the appropriate vocal sound has been inspired, suggested, by the word, that same sound will envelop the word, magnify it, refine and increase the dimension of that very word which was responsible in the first place for its birth. The idea is helped by the sound, and the sound is explained, justified, by the idea: an accomplishment that is physical, psychological, harmonious and perfectly balanced. It is this concordance, this connection, that makes singing fascinating and creates a precious amalgam of a great many abstract and concrete molecules welded together.

Such is my concept of singing. The unusual and challenging implications of this concept must be obvious. I shall try to cast some additional light on all this, not in an attempt to arrive at a solution to the core of the problem, but rather in the hope that deeper scrutiny will clarify a few aspects of it.

I had established a vague plan for this series of lectures, and though I fear it will be difficult for me to follow it, to adhere to it, I will at least make the attempt. And since today's topic is "Why do we sing?" let us seek the answer in popular or folk song.

We need not go back very far. We know that singing played an important role in the ancient civilizations, particularly in Greece. You know that better than others since you were present in this very hall when M. Jean Richepin presented his inspiring lectures on Hellenic religious legends and Hellenic theater. We have learned that singing was important on certain occasions, occasions that were artistic, civic or patriotic. We can also imagine that singing was important in the life of the country people, that it must have accompanied and lightened "the chores and the days," to use the words of Hesiod.

But how did the ancient people sing? About this, we know nothing. When I comment on the history of voice teaching, I shall elaborate a bit on this matter. Today, however, let us consider only spontaneous, popular singing, and let us ask ourselves again: Why do we sing?

We sing for many reasons. We sing because singing is the faithful and docile companion of the lonely, the friend who, in solitude, comforts the sick heart, puts grief to sleep, makes waiting bearable, gives rhythm to labor. It comes or goes at the pleasure of the one who suffers, who works, who grieves. And when, on the other hand, we are joyful, singing is again the friend who shares our happiness, who voices bright joy without bitter reservation. As Nietzsche wrote, "real friendship consists less in sharing the sorrows of those we love than in sharing their joys."

There is, in Taine's *Philosophy of Art,* a beautiful chapter on folk song. There one reads how such a song unfolds, how it is born in the soul and on the lips of the peasant. Read it again. What, for example, does the humble plowman do, the one Voltaire, in one of his few beautiful verses, calls *"Le laboureur ardent qui court avant l'aurore"* ("The earnest plowman who runs before the dawn")?

What does he do when, alone in the furrow behind his plow and his beasts, he feels the need to enliven his monotonous, mechanical work, to ease his efforts, to keep himself company? Does he speak? With whom? With his oxen? He has already exhausted all that he could tell them. Will he talk to himself? The poor fellow! This would require some thought, but thought about what, good heavens? All the thoughts that could arise from his simple and rough mind, his narrow life, his "daily monotony," he has examined and reexamined time and again.

And so, he sings. He sings a plowman's song. Composed by whom? By some other plowman who went before him, who found it even harder to feed his children by his labors, but who was a poet. As a poet, one day he expressed, very simply, his sorrow, and his rare moments of joy, standing in his fields, with their beautiful, golden horizons stretching before him. His were clumsy verses, but strong-flavored and enduring. At first, he may have muttered these verses without singing. But soon this was not enough for him; in the fresh morning air, he felt the need to give them strength, to give them wings, to project them upward towards the clouds, the birds, towards all nature. At this moment, was he to shout? Shouting would have meant greater fatigue, and further, to shout loudly, he would have had to stop walking, to stop working. He was intuitively aware of all this, and so, most naturally, he began to sing. And he soon realized that in singing, he added rhythm to his heavy steps, and strength, spirit and steadiness to his regular exertions. As he sang, he adapted his tune to his movements; he changed it, transformed it, improved it, was elated by it—his song was born.

So this song, repeated by other plowmen and again by other plowmen, will accompany, will brighten the labors of plowmen to come. It is precisely this song that our poor plowman sings this morning.

Very well, but how does he sing it? He has had no singing lessons; he doesn't know that the voice can be placed correctly or incorrectly, that one breathes correctly or wrongly, that one has different registers and timbres. He sings broadly and roughly, taking great gulps of air. And since, in this song, there are embellishments, trills, that he cannot manage, he rushes over them with his voice breaking here and there, producing a *canard*, a "duck squawk." But those very flaws in his singing only add character; and so, if I in turn wish to sing that song, I must strive to imitate them.

* * * * * * * * * *

[At this point in his lecture, the author performed the song he had in mind. Throughout the present volume, a line of asterisks represents a musical example necessarily omitted here.]

This plowman's song most likely goes back to the 17th century; but those sung by Greek plowmen no doubt had a similar origin. Who knows whether, century after century, it is not always the same song, much modified, forever transformed—the song that we hear today in Normandy or Brittany, in Auvergne or Limousin, and the same song the Pelasgians of antiquity heard after Triptolemus taught the arts of agriculture to the people of Eleusis?

At other times, a song is born near a child. The child cries, he is fussy, he refuses to sleep; it is necessary to distract him, to tell him a story, and gradually, in order to gain the child's attention, the mother, who is already poetical because she is a mother caressing her child, becomes a poet. Here and there she rhymes her words as best she can. She adds rhythm, and then, to improve the rhythm of her phrases, she periodically introduces something like a refrain. At first, all this resembles a monotonous chant, but slowly it becomes more precise and turns into a song. And the song that blossoms little by little on the lips of the mother could very well be the *"Trois jeunes princesses couchées sous un pommier . . ."* ("Three young princesses lying under an apple tree . . .").

I will sing it for you, but not as the tender countrywoman would sing as she rocks her child. I will sing it much less simply; a little later, I will tell you why.

* * * * * * * * * *

I have just sung a cradle song, for everything indicates that it is indeed a cradle song: the rhythm, the melodic inflection of the refrain, the general style. And now I will sing another. You will see that only a few notes and a particular timbre suffice to transport us instantly across earth and seas to a distant country, to a foreign land. If, among this audience, there are some who attended my lecture on evocative music two years ago, you may recall my remarks on the incantational power of music. But in singing this second cradle song, my objective is not to demonstrate this power again, but rather to give you a little vocal demonstration; for we should not forget that all this is but a preamble, and we are here to consider singing.

A painter does not prepare his palette in the same way when he is going to paint a dark canvas as when he is going to paint a luminous one. Do not misunderstand me. I am not so ignorant of the painter's technique as to believe that only dark colors are used for a dark picture; and, believe me, in a clear, bright sound, there are often a plenitude of somber undertones, and the reverse is also true. Here we address the whole question of mixed colors or timbres, which we will perhaps have a chance to study later. For the present, it is enough to say there is no doubt that a painter about to depict the interior of a cellar, dimly lit by a smoky lamp, will have less occasion to use transparent, light and brilliant shades than if he intended to paint a sunrise over the ocean. Not only will he prepare his palette differently, but, if I may put it this way, he will also adjust his vision differently; he will eliminate from his visual imagination everything that would work against the ensemble of colors he plans to capture. Without so much as thinking about it, solely from artistic instinct, he will enter a physical and mental state that prefigures either a light vision or a dark one; moreover, the work of his hands will issue from this state he has instinctively entered.

Likewise a composer (also instinctively, of course, because as soon as the will manifests itself, intervenes, one risks falling into pedantry) will choose a specific tone quality for the particular coloring he wishes in a particular song. Each tone, as you know, has its special character, not clearly but indefinably special. Combined and condensed, the diverse tone qualities that emerge in relation to some primordial sound ultimately create a definite impression; the true musician always knows, without any doubts, why he uses this or that timbre. The same is true of orchestration: The musician will not use a trombone to accompany the song of a Sicilian shepherd nor a Basque drum to evoke a funereal ceremony. Likewise, the singer must not only adapt the coloring of his voice to the music he is singing, to what he seeks to express, but must also adapt his diction to that end. Like his voice, the very words he pronounces must be imbued, saturated, with the thought he wishes to convey: The openness of the vowels, the greater or lesser emphasis in the projection of the consonants, the greater or lesser insistence on nasal or dental sounds—all this is important, but one must not appear to think about it. Indeed one must not think about it; it must come about quite naturally, as if in response to an irresistible interior impulse.

A moment ago, as I was singing the plowman's song, you noted that I attempted to imitate the voice of the peasant, singing in the open air against the wind. In the following song, goodness knows, I sang like anyone else. We were at home, in France, in a familiar landscape. But now I must change my voice; this song is a Greek one. And here are the words: "Sleep, my daughter, sleep. I

34

will give you the city of Alexandria in sugar, Cairo in rice, and Constantinople, so that you may reign for three years."

How old is this song? I do not know. Bourgault-Ducoudray found it at Smyrna. It is powerfully evocative; it is impossible to listen to it without catching a glimpse, as if through a haze of gold dust, of minarets and scintillating cupolas, a grand mirage of the Orient. But the impression would be infinitely less vivid if I sang this song with a Western voice. If I wish, with the first measure, to transport you there, I must sing the song as it was sung by the prince or the beggar-poet who created it. Of course I will take care to stress those magnificent words: *Alexandria, Constantinople*, for in themselves, they convey something magical. Not only is it imperative that I "see," that I have before my eyes all that I wish to show you; not only is it imperative that I become an Oriental, indolent, dreamy, still (all this is the mental, psychical work of singing), but I must also be able to control the vocal mechanisms that permit me to portray an Oriental voice. I will lower the soft palate so that the air flowing out of my lungs will direct the sound not entirely through my mouth but also through my nose in order to obtain some resonance in my nasal fossae. Moreover, I will sometimes pull my tongue back towards the back of my throat to give my voice a guttural tint.

So much for the timbre. And now, for the sound itself. First, I will often attack it from below, according to Oriental custom. And then, Oriental people always trill slightly in their singing—their sound is rarely even and round but has something of a trembling quality—so I shall do my best, through light and rapid contractions of my larynx, to impart to the sound this special characteristic. The small groups of notes I shall perform with that particular brusqueness of Oriental people, which makes them almost "squawk" on such embellishments. In addition, I will remain in the same register, for Orientals, unless they are expert singers, do not pay much attention to that matter, and logically so; they simply "push" towards the high notes, up to the extreme limits of the register in which they are singing. Lastly, in the final exhalation of each note, I will remember not to prolong the note or the breath, but instead stop the exhalation by a stroke of the glottis.

* * * * * * * * * *

Another reason for singing is the desire to secure a greater permanence, a persistence, for one's words. For example, one of the most frequent themes in popular or folk songs is the farewell of a young man to his beloved. Why is this young man not content to tell his sorrow, to pour out his emotions, in simple words? He sings instead. He does so because the melody will etch itself more deeply in the memory of his beloved; the words will find in the melody a sort of armor against the erosion of memory which proceeds slowly but surely day after day, hour after hour, indeed each minute that goes by. Simply spoken, those words of parting, however tender, might at length be forgotten by the one to whom they were addressed; but the music gives them the powerful possibility of longer life, a thoroughgoing and indelible virtue. Thus we have another reason why one might sing: to endow words or thoughts with a semblance of eternity. Just as we engrave inscriptions on stone or marble, we engrave them in music. And is it not wonderful that such an impalpable and insubstantial means as music can serve to transmit ideas, give them life, permanence and significance across the ages?

How did those moving legends, those great epics of antiquity, reach us if not through the voice of the bards, of the rhapsodists, and then of the people who remembered their songs? Do we not find in the plaintive ballads of the Middle Ages innumerable accounts of warriors' exploits, veritable chronicles of war, born most probably from soldiers' improvisations during a march or around a campfire in the evening?

Such, for example, is the horrific account of King Renaud:

Le roi Renaud de guerre vint,
Tient ses entrailles dans sa main;
Sa mère était sur les créneaux
Pour voir venir son fils Renaud.

King Renaud returned from war,
Holding his entrails in his hands;
His mother stood on the battlements
To see her son Renaud returning.

"Marching soldiers"—I spoke these words, and they brought to mind still another reason for singing. There is nothing quite like singing to revive the spirit and energize a troop of tired soldiers. During the first two or three hours of a march in the morning, after a good night's rest, soldiers seldom sing. But, as soon as their legs tell them they have marched many miles, the singing begins. At the first signs of fatigue, which adds weight to their packs and guns, three or four among them begin to hum. Soon others add their voices, then others, until before long the entire company sing in full voice at the top of their lungs. The march improves immediately, becomes more regular, precise, rhythmical; and at the same time, their feeling of fatigue is reduced as the words of their songs turn their minds from other concerns. In fact, soldiers' songs typically consist of an enormous number of verses, each dealing with a specific episode, which, when linked together, complete a tale. The verses of such stories must necessarily be sung in their proper order, and the small effort of attention this demands will divert the mind from fatigue. To be truthful, I wish that the words of these songs were less coarse than they usually are—there are exceptions, and sometimes the words are thoroughly charming— but the tunes are generally quite pretty.

Recently, as I fulfilled my military obligation, I could not help but notice that many of the tunes I heard around me were ancient tunes, perpetuated in this manner by many generations of soldiers. Some of these songs, from the 17th and 18th centuries, were truly delightful, with brisk and sometimes ingenious rhythms. I observed the soldiers while they were singing (for when one loves singing as I do, one neglects no opportunity for learning), and I was intrigued to discover that they all sang quite well. Obviously, they did not all have a special talent for singing. But, first of all, they were singing loudly, and as you are well aware, it is much easier to sing loudly and without nuance than to sing softly with various colorings of the voice. Furthermore, walking requires a continuous movement of the body which prevents the muscles from tightening up; and those among you, Mesdemoiselles, who are taking voice lessons, know that one of the greatest enemies of good tone production is stiffness. Finally, the weight of their sacks pulls their shoulders down and back and thus prevents the contraction of the clavicles, which is another serious obstacle to good singing. You can see that my time in the service was not wasted!

Beyond the need to inspire marching spirit, there is still another reason to sing: to inspire dancing spirit. In the countryside—and it is the same for the most distant epoch as for today—how is it possible to dance together gaily without music? When one is far from the village, in the fields, and between stints of hard work, there is not always a flute, a violin, a bagpipe, at hand. And so one sings, and, contrary to what I was describing a moment ago, it is now the words, gradually recalled by one person or another, that enliven and strengthen the singing. Countless lively round dances were thus born; free, joyful, unburdened, in keeping with the natural movements of the body, similar to those of young animals and blithe nymphs; bounding, leaping dances having nothing to do with that anxious and cheerless staggering, that dance of intoxicated webfeet, ridiculous and lugubrious at the same time, the kind of dancing in fashion today.

Singers who have reached a reasonable level of vocal skill should sing every day for a period of time, first walking, then dancing to some particularly rhythmic music, without employing too much voice, but pronouncing words, and preferably a great number of words. By so doing they will acquire the habit of singing rhythmically (which most seldom do, for the lack of a sense of rhythm is a plague among singers) and also of communicating the diverse sentiments conveyed by the words through a variety of vocal inflections, variously accenting the syllables and, if necessary, altering facial expressions and breathing according to the demands of the text: all this *without changing the tempo of the music.*

c&o

When all is said and done, however, it is love that provides the greatest impetus for singing; it is love that has inspired the great majority of folk songs. Desire, expectation, joy, deception, jealousy, regret, hope, spite—all these sentiments born of love are the wellsprings of invention for the soul which seeks expression. And since words are too short, too dry and above all too few among simple men and women, the very people who create folk songs (and who, precisely because they are simple, are more apt to experience strong emotions and more inclined to reveal them)— in short, since words alone are not enough for them, they sing the words to give them force and emotion.

"Mona,"[3] one of the most poetical songs of Lower Brittany, evokes the sad plight of a young country girl abandoned and forgotten by her beloved. Here we are very close to nature, to the land. If one knows the techniques of singing, this is not the occasion to use them. Now one must appear to sing because it is impossible to do otherwise, because the heart is overflowing. You will object that it is not Mona herself who sings, but another who describes her weeping among the willows by the river. This is true, but this other who tells the story performs, so to speak, the role of the chorus in Greek theater: She deeply identifies with the heroine, she feels and suffers with her. And, I repeat, since the song places us in the midst of Brittany, this narrator, this humble bard who must sing, must have a feeling for this land, must know the melancholy of its moors, the gentle, vast undulations of its bitter landscape. Above all, what is needed here is a plain voice, devoid of roundness or resonance; a naïve and plaintive voice producing mournful tones, saturated with melancholy, with lingering extensions of phrases, reflecting the quiet and gloomy sameness of the life led by the people: fishermen and wives of fishermen, resigned to the passiveness of waiting and waiting.

* * * * * * * * * *

This sort of plainness of the voice gives to the words and what they conjure in the mind a rough simplicity equivalent to that which M. Cottet bestows on the people in his Breton paintings. The dialogue in the little song that I will now sing for you, "Ma Douce Annette,"[4] is charming, naïve, tender and soft. But as you know, simple folk are timid, especially in matters of love, and the Breton peasants more so than most. During this little dialogue, in which we hear first the young man and then the young girl, one must not use nuances or accentuate this or that word. The two speak together softly, their eyes lowered. The young couple summon the image of a primitive painting: He holds her hand, and he is greatly embarrassed by his own audacity. Think back to the sailors in the novels of Loti,[5] how they tremble, how awkward they become when addressing their fiancée, the one "their heart loves so dearly," as the old song says.

When singing, one must seek inspiration everywhere; singing, to use a pedantic word, must be filled with "references"; it must not flow out of the larynx before it has sojourned not only in the heart but especially in the brain, where it takes on a multiplicity of ideas, thoughts, intentions, of which the listener will perceive only the vestiges, but the absence of these vestiges is quickly apparent when the listener is neither moved nor charmed.

I said earlier that I would not sing the cradle song about the *"trois jeunes princesses"* as the countrywoman who composed it would. Indeed, how is one to sing folk songs? Country people who sing them (frequently with a lovely voice and great simplicity) always sing mechanically, while performing a duty or task, while rocking a child, spinning, knitting, or doing rustic chores like mowing, gleaning, peeling vegetables, harvesting, weaving baskets and so on. As a consequence, the singing borrows a regular cadence from the manual or bodily rhythm; the words are pronounced in a uniform and monotonous way. If a story unfolds in the song—a tale of love, a heroic or simple story—the singer, in his interpretation, does not try to emphasize this or that detail of the story; instead, he sings most naturally, as the song comes to him, always in the same rhythmic manner and always with the same tone quality. Nonetheless, the setting adds considerable poetry to this sort of singsong chant. The singer is surrounded by sky, forest, valley, or by the modest furnishings of a home; the setting is natural, serious or merry, gray or multicolored, supplied by the countryside, by life itself. His singing seems to come from the earth and can be compared to the cries of the cicada, to bird calls, to the sounds of the breeze passing over the thatched cottage. Against this varied background, which creates an atmosphere often noble and touching, the words stand out without nuances but clearly, and the full meaning of the song is realized in the calm of the natural surroundings. The song produces its legendary effect, plaintive, sentimental or picturesque, because it is performed in the environment that witnessed its birth, the environment that gave it birth.

We cannot replicate this setting when we sing a folk song, accompanying ourselves on a piano, surrounded by *salon* furniture or in a concert hall. In these circumstances, we must resort to some kind of artifice, or, if you will, to art, to compensate for the poetical contribution the peasant singer finds in the world around him. Sometimes one can create that illusion by imitating the voice of the peasant, by adopting, for the sake of the interpretation, an untrained, monotonous voice, be it mournful or joyful, but a voice unconcerned with its own shape, with employing subtle inflections for the sake of the words being sung.

Other times, in contrast, it is necessary to extract from the song all the poetry, all the style, all the movement that is in it, with the help of diction, a few pauses, some "holding back" or some acceleration as suggested by good taste and inspired by emotion. Or if one is relating a drama or a romance, one should not hesitate to resort to certain dramatic means, used with moderation and discretion. I do not mean that in such a way one can recreate the exact impression made by the song when sung in its own setting, in its time and by the voice the song requires in a real sense; but one can, at least, give the song a poetical effect, or draw from it a portion of emotion.

[1] Taken from M. Isnardon's treatise on singing.

[2] *Ibid.*

[3] Bourgault-Ducoudray: *Chansons de la Basse-Bretagne*.

[4] *Ibid.*

[5] [Pierre Loti (1850–1923), a major French writer. His novel *Mme Chrysanthème* formed the subject of Messager's opera by that title (1893).]

II

How Do We Sing?

Mesdames, Mesdemoiselles, Messieurs,

Eight days ago, we discussed the principle that, in my
opinion, must govern the esthetic of singing. We concluded
that it consists of an indissoluble synthesis of psychological elements and physical means, of a close association of speech and
sound, that is to say, of the word and of singing as such. Now I
would like to take up several specific matters relating to these two
distinct domains: the voice, which is to say, singing; the word,
which is to say, the soul and spirit. At our last meeting, we made
several excursions into the realms of the sentimental and the picturesque; today we shall focus our attention on certain mechanical
questions. But before I proceed, I must reemphasize that it is
impossible to completely separate the physical realization of
singing from the inner forces that direct and control it.

Have you ever visited a glass manufacturing plant? Were you
in Venice, for example, and did you ask your gondolier to stop at

the Murano factory? If you did, if you wandered as I did around the fiery furnaces over which men bent laboriously, their faces attentive, their skilled hands in constant motion, their fingers and wrists, surprisingly supple, performing tasks of the most delicate and rarefied nature—then you have a fairly good idea of what working with a voice should be, an idea, rather, of the very creation of incandescent song.

The glass, glowing red, made luminous and supple by the heat, is forcefully seized with tongs, but in such a way as to inflict no damage. In his right hand, the workman holds other tongs; these are diverse in shape and complicated to handle. With this second instrument, he works the glass he is holding with his left hand. With extraordinary deftness (for he must act while the glass is molten), he subjects it to infinite manipulations: He twirls it into spirals; stretches it; flattens it; forms it into a ball and then, from the ball, draws out slender, glowing strips and shapes them in their turn, imposing upon the soft, malleable material, curves, protuberances and hollows, giving it the most varied, the most whimsical forms as it glows red-hot all the while. Not only does he give the molten glass a form, he also gives it color, reaching into the boiling, bubbling vats to draw out pigments of various hues. He applies those delicately chosen nuances to the shape he has prepared to receive them.

Barely has he completed his task of modeling and coloring when the glass begins to harden. Iridescent flashes sparkle in its transparent veins, projecting a sudden, superb brilliance or an indescribable fusion of delicate, light tints: It is a flower, a crystalline butterfly, a flaming sphere, a luminous stream immobilized in a bizarre and charming arabesque, a ray of light, a still, pearl-white pond. The forms, the colors, are infinite and infinitely varied, and this miraculous result has been realized through quick, sure work in which diverse and often opposing processes combine in a single act performed upon an amorphous and transmutable material.

Adelina Patti, Italian soprano (1843–1919). Reproduced from the Collections of the Library of Congress.

I have never observed the marvelous process of glassmaking without thinking about the singer's art at the moment of singing. The work of the singer, unlike that of other artists, is not surrounded by mystery: It takes place publicly, in full view, observed by the very audience for whom it is intended, by the very ones it is meant to surprise, attract, charm.

The singer creates the material he uses, shapes it and exhibits it at the same moment. He is the only artist subjected to such a condition: The painter, the composer, the writer, indeed all other artists accomplish their tasks in solitude, in silence and serenity, as inspiration strikes them. They can start over, correct and regulate themselves; and their finished work does not appear before those who will judge it until it has come to completion under many circumstances favorable to perfection, including prolonged reflection and stubborn work.

Such is not the case for the singer: It is while we listen to him, at the very moment, the very second, when we judge him, that he creates and gives shape to his material. That shape must be definitive—he has no time to modify it, to transform it; the audience hears it just as it was created and without the slightest delay. He cannot afford to hesitate, he cannot "repent," as the painters say, or rectify his mistakes. Within an imperceptible space of time, with prodigious rapidity and through instinctive skill (into which several physiological acts must join), the singer fashions his material. He shapes it, gives it a plastic beauty (for there is much that is plastic in singing), a sonorous beauty, but he must also infuse it with emotion, poetry, thought. At the very moment the voice blossoms forth—just as the singer gives it birth in the recesses of his lungs, by his larynx, palate, lips—his brain and his heart must supply this intangible material (for the singer's material is readily dissolved, an abstract substance, so to speak), his brain and his heart must bestow upon this impalpable, imponderable thing which is the sound, enough thought, enough psychic virtue, that this sound so subtly produced will move, exalt, desolate, enrapture or intoxicate by the combined effect of the music and the word.

But while glass will harden into a tangible, enduring object, the sound, only just perceived, disappears. The glassmaker, after his rapid series of manipulations, can at least contemplate the result of his work to his heart's content, drink it in with his eyes, admire or criticize it and, if necessary, destroy it and start again. The singer has no such privilege. What he has produced is irrevocable: He cannot make it disappear because its memory lingers on, intangible yet fixed and, so to speak, hanging in the ether. The singer cannot destroy it, for what he has created exists no more. Singing, precisely because it is ephemeral, is, in some way, eternal.

Indeed, the singer's task is not only one of the most difficult, but one of the most trying that exist; not at all because of the great muscular strength it requires, but because it demands the focused coordination of the entire organism, subordinated to the brain directing and controlling it. The period of time required to sing a phrase is really very short. When I sing:

Nuit se‿rei‿ne,   O nuit bien fai‿san‿te!

just that, no more than that, it seems that I have accomplished nothing extraordinary. This is so when we look at the matter superficially; but, upon detailed analysis, here is exactly what I have done in the few seconds it took to sing that phrase: I have set up (probably quite unconsciously, but simply out of physiological habit) my vocal organs, which are quite numerous—my diaphragm, lungs, larynx, palate, tongue, and jaw—in their respective and appropriate positions. All the muscles of my body played a part, however small, in this work. First, I produced the breath necessary to emit a few sounds. I have imposed upon this breath a large number of resonant vibrations, thus forming a continuous sound which may have been imperfect due to my own deficiencies but which, if it had emerged as I wished it, would have offered, thanks to certain extremely tenuous combinations of mixed vowels, a smooth, round, full, brilliant sound. That sound was already a complex physical phenomenon, but it would have amounted to very little had I not added the *meaning* expressed by these words: "*Nuit sereine! O nuit bienfaisante!*" ("Serene night! O beneficent night!"). And those words would have meant nothing had I not said them in such a way as to evoke in your mind the calm, the peace, the soft, pleasurable feeling of a summer night, and had I not added to this invocation a slightly reverent inflection, a prayerful modulation, for it is a prayer.

Thus it was essential that, at the time of this physical yet delicate and mysterious coordination of the muscles and the viscera, I superimposed the intellectual, the abstract and, we can almost say, supernatural input of thought and feeling. It should be evident that, in those few seconds, I expended a good bit of my inmost energy. Now consider the expenditure of self required for a singer (who sings well) to perform, not a fragment with piano accompaniment, but a scene, an act, an entire opera, accompanied by a large orchestra.

Certainly, the art of singing is one of the most complex that exist; it is unstable ground of which the singer must know not only the consistency, the depth, the contour and composition, but onto which he must venture boldly, seeking a sort of perpetual balance, holding himself ready to overcome any accident of terrain, to change his tactics in the face of unforeseen circumstances. It is an art that should be tackled only by those who possess a profound desire to study with unremitting seriousness, application and perseverance. It is this solemnity, this meditative quality, this fierce will and burning, passionate persistence that are notably lacking in almost all our singers today.

❦

A singer never finishes learning: The progress of a singer who works at his art ends only with his life; the loss of his voice does not bring his work to a halt, for the real work of singing is mental. However, most of today's singers think about singing only as they begin to sing; then, stricken with anxiety, they think about specific notes they fear or about a certain breath they must not forget. Since they have neglected to carry on this unceasing, mostly mental, vocal preparation, their delivery has never become automatic; and so, as soon as they start to sing, they become so preoccupied with their voice that their brain has no room for the thoughts that should really fill it. Yes, it is true that singing, above all, must engage the *mind.*

There is a saying by Garat[1] that is touching indeed for those who understand and cultivate singing. After a glorious career such as few singers have known, Garat, grown old, his voice gone, was asked by a friend if he still occasionally tried to sing. He replied, "No, that is impossible; but my mind sings in silence, *and I have never sung better.*"

I recently asked Mme Lilli Lehmann why she never sang a certain Beethoven composition which I thought would be most appropriate for her.[2] She answered: "I have worked on it for seventeen years; but I still don't have it right!"

And so, one can only shrug one's shoulders in the face of the vanity of those who are convinced they have nothing more to learn once they are able to spit out a high B-flat or to go beyond a few low notes with a minimum of effort. Their attitude would be laughable if music did not suffer so by virtue of such insolence. Their presumption, however, is a lesser shortcoming than the ignorance of some music critics and the frivolity of the public;

their praise and applause encourage these miserable singers to persist in their laziness and infatuation with themselves.

Let us leave this sad subject.

Naturally, I have no intention of giving a lecture on physiology; but all the same, I cannot speak of singing without the aid of anatomical charts. Incidentally, I am amazed that singing teachers do not use a simple, well-made model of the respiratory and vocal apparatus in their teaching, for they could indicate with precision many things that are most difficult to convey to someone who has no idea of the shape or function of the organs involved in singing. I should add that, among the great singers, some are totally ignorant of their singing mechanisms. Mme Lilli Lehmann, who is the most erudite singer of our time, says in her treatise, after a meticulous and masterly description of certain aspects of the vocal mechanism:

> Adelina Patti was the greatest Italian singer of our time. Everything about her singing was absolutely beautiful, impeccable and pure; her voice resonated like a bell and left the impression of continued ringing long after its final vibrations. However, she could give no explanation of her art, and, when questioned on the matter, she would reply: "I have no idea how I do it."[3]

The fact is that Mme Patti's vocal instinct was such that it encompassed the whole gamut of the singing process. One could not hope to find among all singers the same degree of talent as Mme Patti's; but if one has no vocal instinct whatsoever, one will never succeed in singing well, no matter how hard one works at it. One must have talent for singing, as one must have talent for mathematics or painting. The day when this reality is acknowledged, many cruel disappointments will be avoided.

Vocal talent is independent of the voice, just as eloquence is independent of pronunciation and choreographic genius is independent of bodily beauty. Determination can accomplish almost anything in matters of singing if it is guided by vocal instinct; otherwise it remains useless. The voice has importance, but a secondary one. A beautiful voice is not necessarily compatible with vocal instinct. A beautiful voice may lead anywhere, but we err in believing that a beautiful voice automatically makes a singer. This is equivalent to saying that a woman with beautiful legs must necessarily become a great dancer. Vocal talent can, in a strict sense, succeed without a great voice (at least in the realm of connoisseurs), but *a great voice cannot succeed without vocal talent* (cannot at any rate charm people of taste).

The foremost vocal motor, the absolute wellspring of singing, is breathing. The originators of methods, the voice teachers, are correct in attaching great importance to breathing. However, they are wrong, it seems to me, when they try to impose, each according to his or her own system, a single, invariable way of breathing. All the treatises on singing should include a complete and carefully outlined list of the different approaches to breathing. The student, presumably one who is serious and studious, should choose for himself, after long and numerous experiments, the way of singing that is best for him, not only in relation to the particulars of his own lungs, ribs and larynx, but also to the instinctive movements of his muscular and nervous systems, to his general bearing, to his entire physical makeup. In fact, it is less a question of learning to breathe in a certain manner than of learning to control the way one breathes naturally, and to use this knowledge methodically, in keeping with one's own vocal situation.

Breathing is the essence of singing—but let me make myself clear. There are two kinds of breathing: physiological breathing (which constitutes the foundation, the basis of singing) and expressive breathing. Let us turn first to breathing of the former kind.

Physiological breathing consists of two movements: inhalation and exhalation. It is not difficult to inhale, to store a certain quantity of air; but it can be very difficult to exhale. Here the difficulty lies in the necessity of releasing only the quantity of breath required to sustain the sound. The voice, as you know, is nothing more than breath coming out of the lungs, which the larynx transforms into sound through the vibration of the vocal cords.

These, in turn, are rather thick cartilages which in no way resemble cords; there are two of them. Some writers make a distinction between their lower and upper parts by calling them "vocal cords" and "false vocal cords," respectively. But, basically, if we want to simplify matters, there are two vocal cords, contrary to most people's belief that the larynx is shaped like a harp or a guitar. A singer told me one day: "I have a terrible case of the flu, *all my vocal cords* are affected!"

By their vibrations, the two vocal cords transform into sound the breath that passes between them. This movement of air would not exist without the act of breathing. Therefore, once again, breathing is the very foundation of singing.

There are many ways of breathing. Rossini supposedly said that there were two: the good and the bad. But this is making light of the matter, and we are far too serious for that! Indeed, there are several ways of breathing; there are even innumerable ways. But we will be content to identify only three of them.

There is what we commonly and awkwardly call "abdominal" breathing; this is effected by lowering the diaphragm, which allows the air to penetrate to the very bottom of the lungs. There is also "thoracic" breathing, which is carried out by expanding the rib cage. And, finally, there is breathing that takes place at the top of the lungs. But this particular type, "wounded bird" breathing, is to be avoided. Many women use it either due to laziness or due to the restrictions of the corset (nowadays almost totally abolished), which for years made it impossible for them to expand the thorax, so that they developed a habit of breathing by simply raising the chest and even, slightly, the shoulders, a technique which is most unsightly and also extremely tiring.

Abdominal breathing is excellent, especially for the theater. Breathing from the rib cage also has advantages. I will go further: I even believe that "wounded bird" breathing has its usefulness, and that we need to know how to breathe in every way, using each of these methods according to circumstances.

Above all, breathing must be easy or, at least, must give that impression; it should not attract any more attention than it does in conversation. When we speak, we breathe, for if we do not breathe, we die; however, we do not *think about* breathing. When we give a speech, when we are in the heat of a discussion which leads us to pronounce a considerable quantity of words in succession, we do not say: "Attention, I must breathe or else I will suffocate." Rarely do we say, for example: "Monsieur, I was very sorry to learn that Mademoiselle, your daughter, is not well, but I know that she is recuperating, and I hope (*breath*) that she will soon be up and about."

Nevertheless, we breathe. When? Where? No one knows. The same must be the case while singing; our breathing must seem natural to the listener. Some people breathe very little while singing. I believe that they are right: Too many breaths do not facilitate singing and may in fact hamper it. But some masters (M. Fauré,[4] for example, in his very interesting book *La Voix et le Chant* [*The Voice and Singing*]), recommend breathing frequently, taking only a bit of air each time. I have no doubt that M. Fauré is right. Yet it seems to me that singing constantly interrupted by breathing does not truly resemble speech (and let us remember that our wish, above all, is for singing to be simply a more beautiful form of speech, ever inspired by the spoken word).

If I breathe infrequently (I do not offer myself as a model but simply as an example), I hold back my breath or, at least, let it escape in minimal quantities. Moreover, I do not breathe in only one way. Occasionally, after having contracted my diaphragm and inhaled deeply, I "lock" myself—to use Mme Lehmann's expression—upon my upper ribs as upon two supports, and I exhale slowly. I then feel my diaphragm slowly returning to its normal position; but I have the impression that the air comes out in tiny quantities, and that my diaphragm moves most carefully.

Other times, I realize that after inhaling in the usual way, I relax the muscles of my diaphragm, so that air flows out much more smoothly.

Still other times, I breathe without pulling in my stomach even slightly, yet somehow I find that I have a sufficient quantity of air to sustain my singing for a relatively long time. An unbelievably small amount of air is required to sustain a sound.

Notice, for example, that the flame of a match or a candle barely flickers as I exhale in singing:

Certainly, if I pronounced such consonants as *p, f, m, s, c, z* or *d*, the flame would move, but that is caused by the thrust of air produced by the consonants, and not by my singing breath. If I say: "*Quand la fleur du soleil, la rose de Lahor*" ("When the flower of the sun, the rose of Lahore"), the flame will move at "*Quand*," "*fleur*," "*soleil*," and so on. But if I sing the same phrase omitting the consonants by saying: "*And, a, eur, u, o, eil*" instead of "*Quand la fleur du soleil*," the flame will not move.

It is not solely by singing an isolated sound that I can leave the flame motionless. Here is a short excerpt from Handel in which the same result is obtained in spite of the sinuous arabesque of the melodic line:

Très lent

Glide thou like a crys - tal flood, glide thou like a

Fragment chanté sans

crys - tal flood, glide

respirer devant une bougie allumée sans que

la flamme oscille

thou like a crys - tal flood.

The excerpt marked with a line above the upmost staff is sung without taking a breath and without causing the candle flame to flicker.

It is well established that in breathing, it is absolutely essential to let no more air escape than is necessary to supply the sound. My impression is that teachers are too concerned with inhalation and not enough so with exhalation. Not only does careful and parsimonious breath control lead to phrasing devoid of jerks and jolts; it also makes it possible to shade the sound infinitely, to increase it from an almost inaudible *pianissimo* to a brilliant *fortissimo*. In this way, we can select from the rich palette of nuances the one best suited for the particular note and word; we can shape the intensity of the sound easily and with considerable refinement, which is completely impossible when we allow the breath to emerge rapidly and, especially, when we have not held enough in reserve.

Once again, singing is breath imbued with sound. It is the power behind our breath, the amplitude that we give it with the larynx, soft palate, tongue and lips, the innumerable modifications that we bring to it—it is all this that causes us to sing well or badly. Do not believe that one can sing well and breathe badly; this is impossible, illogical, and credible only to those who have never sung. (And be forewarned that there are many such among our teachers.)

I have already mentioned that breathing is not only a physical necessity, it not only sustains the sound and controls its proportions, but it also offers singers a very important means of expression. I need not repeat that when we sing, we must pronounce the words distinctly, perfectly understandably, each with its proper spacing and duration. The objects and scenes they evoke, the thoughts they convey, must confer upon them a special color and accent.

But in addition, through sensitive, hardly noticeable

interruptions, through scarcely perceptible or, on the contrary, extended pauses, words must be harmoniously grouped and balanced, gathered in diverse clusters that make feeling manifest, that grant description its full and effective force. It is breathing that brings all this about. One phrase must be uttered in a single outflow, without the slightest interruption; another must be broken up systematically or irregularly, divided into parts of different lengths. One word must be highlighted, emphasized, presented in isolation, while another word, on the contrary, must slip away, fade into shadow, disappear in the haze of the breath. One breath must be imperceptible to the listener; another must be obvious, strongly marked, almost noisy, as expression demands. It is one's taste and personality that determine all this. What is necessary is that the listener never realize that *we take a breath because we are out of air*. When the physical need to breathe presents itself, it must always be justified, made acceptable; it must always seem to be required by the meaning of the words or by the feeling.

Routine and habit are responsible for the fact that listeners are not generally surprised by certain arbitrary breaths that would astonish them in spoken language. This is a centuries-old tradition of which singers take advantage. I believe that we should, as much as possible, abstain from the practice: We can revivify and restore freshness to many selections grown dreary and worn through a long habit of mediocrity—we can give new life to the music—by restoring breathing that is consistent with good sense. In music of the 17th and 18th centuries, in which long vocalises frequently appear (you noticed one in the selection from Handel I sang a moment ago), we have come to tolerate some very arbitrary breaths, in the middle of a phrase, before an essential word, sometimes even in the middle of a word if the word is part of a long vocalise. But I truly believe we can almost always avoid such unnatural breaks. In a short Handel aria that I will sing for you— and which, I hasten to add, is not among the most difficult—there are two or three points where a rather long breath is required, but where I nonetheless manage to breathe in a way which is not contrary to good sense.

For example:

To sing this excerpt in one breath, one has only to carefully control the outflow of air and, towards the end, when the supply is almost exhausted, to make a *crescendo* (perfectly justified by the thought of joy, exuberance), which, by collecting all the remaining breath and spending it on a few notes, does not convey to the listener any impression of choking for air.

Many composers, including some of the greatest, do not give a thought to breathing as they compose. Many vocal masterpieces present the performer with real challenges in the management of the breath. One of Fauré's most beautiful *mélodies*, "Le Parfum impérissable," presents some quite unusual problems. I will sing it for you, not in a single sweep, but stopping here and there to focus on those difficulties and to suggest solutions.

Indeed, this is one of the composer's most beautiful songs, marking the transition from the Fauré of "La Pavane avec choeurs" to that of "La Chanson d'Eve." Clearly characteristic of the composer's genius, it bears the inimitable mark of his unique musical language, so penetrating, always exquisitely and richly configured. This *mélodie*, by progressive and increasing waves, creates an emotion which, in spite of the strict economy of the melodic expression, attains at the end an extraordinary intensity. The verses of the *mélodie*, by Leconte de Lisle, are as follows:

Le Parfum impérissable

Quand la fleur du soleil, la rose de Lahor,
De son âme odorante a rempli goutte à goutte
La fiole d'argile | *ou de cristal* | *ou d'or,*
Sur le sable qui brûle | *on peut l'épandre toute.*

Les fleuves et la mer inonderaient en vain
Ce sanctuaire étroit qui la tint enfermée,
Il garde en se brisant son arôme divin
Et sa poussière heureuse | *en reste parfumée.*

Puisque par la blessure ouverte de mon coeur
Tu t'écoules de même, | *ô céleste liqueur,*
Inexprimable amour qui m'enflammait pour elle!

Qu'il lui soit pardonné, que mon mal soit béni!
Par delà l'heure humaine et le temps infini
Mon coeur est embaumé d'une odeur immortelle!

Leconte de Lisle

The Imperishable Perfume

When the flower of the sun, the rose of Lahore,
Has filled with its fragrant soul drop by drop,
The vial of clay or crystal or gold,
It can all be poured out on the burning sand.

In vain the rivers and the sea wash over
The narrow sanctuary which confines it still,
Though broken it keeps its divine aroma
And its blissful dust retains the sweet perfume.

Since through the open wound of my heart
You likewise flow, O celestial nectar,
Inexpressible love for her that inflamed me!

May she be forgiven, may my sorrow be blessed!
Beyond the human span and infinite time,
My heart is embalmed with an immortal fragrance!

Let us look at the first lines:

Quand la fleur du soleil, la rose de Lahor,
De son âme odorante a rempli goutte à goutte,
La fiole d'argile ou de cristal ou d'or,

As you can see, the phrase is long; and it is rendered even longer by the music, which is slow, poised. Where can I breathe in this phrase? Evidently and logically, I could breathe at the comma that follows "*Quand la fleur du soleil,*" and again at the comma that follows "*la rose de Lahor.*" To do so would be correct—and silly. Yet it would be foolhardy to attempt to sing this verse, and the two that follow, in single, sweeping breaths: This would be almost impossible and would give the audience the impression of fatigue and anguish. Therefore, by virtue of a principle that I shall try to clarify a bit later (and which, I believe, has never been formulated before), I shall breathe after "*Lahor*"; but this breath is permissible only *if I justify it by giving the impression of saying these words in parenthesis: "la rose de Lahor."* I must therefore detach these words from the first part of the phrase, and since I do not want to breathe after "*Quand la fleur du soleil*" (because it would be childish and would break up the musical phrase), I will do this:

Let us continue:

De son âme odorante a rempli goutte à goutte
La fiole d'argile ou de cristal ou d'or,

60

Here the only place I could breathe without offending reason is between "*rempli*" and "*goutte à goutte,*" which would, nevertheless, imply another breath before "*La fiole.*" But this would be abominable, almost ridiculous; it would seem to be panting, and also, that resumption of singing on the word "*La fiole*"—in short, I do not know why, but it is impossible. It is therefore essential to sing without interruption:

> *De son âme odorante a rempli goutte à goutte*
> *La fiole d'argile*

Now, strictly speaking, you may breathe; but then you must breathe again *without wishing to do so* after "*ou de cristal,*" because if you did not, if you did not feign a breath at these two points *for the sole purpose of emphasizing an enumeration,* it would be obvious that you inserted a breath after "*argile*" *because you needed to take a breath.* In that case, once again, you would have to sing "*a rempli goutte à goutte La fiole d'argile* (breath) *ou de cristal* (breath) *ou d'or.*" Truly, this is a complicated affair! Is it not more natural, straightforward and beautiful to sing:

Here, take a deep breath and sing without interruption:

Indeed, by taking no breath after *"brrûle"* (for two *r*'s are needed) and by placing between *"brûle"* and *"on"* an *"h"* accentuated by a slight outflow of breath, you add life and realism to the image of that essence which flows out of the vial, leaving its traces on the sand—particularly if you take care to give full value to the nasal *"pan"* in *"épandre"* and to deemphasize the F-sharp of *"toute"* by attacking it slightly from below. (Of course, these little tricks must be used with extreme discretion and tact. When I sing, the audience should not even detect them; in seeking to explain them, I exaggerate.)

Les   fleu - ves   et la mer____ i - non.de -
. raient en vain Ce sanctuaire étroit qui la tint enfermé.e

It seems out of the question, you will agree, to breathe between *"en vain"* and *"Ce sanctuaire"*; yet one can, by virtue of a principle that I shall explain later, breathe after *"Les fleuves et la mer"* in order to sing, afterwards, in one breath, *"inonderaient en vain Ce sanctuaire,"* and so on. Yet to me it seems preferable to sing these two verses in one extended stretch—if, of course, one can do it. Let us continue.

Il garde en se bri - sant _____ son a - rô - me di - vin
Et sa poussière heureuse en res - te parfu - mé - e. __

To be sure, one should breathe only after *"divin."* Let me offer a few comments on this last verse. If you sing the verse in a smooth voice, very *legato,* with an even sound, stressing the sinuous elegance of the musical phrase, it will be well done: The words will receive their due, the poetical thought will be readily perceived. But the metaphor will not be *visible;* the meaning will be there but not the image, the thought but not the feeling.

To sing this passage so that it conveys the proper feeling, sing it as follows: *"Et sa poussière heureuse en"* in a soft voice, but firmly supported and slightly *crescendo.* On *"reste,"* a sudden *pianissimo, not obtained by a sudden* diminuendo, *but by totally dropping the support and strongly releasing the breath on the* r; (the *e* in *"res-te"* fully open). On *"par,"* slowly resume the support, strengthen it by means of the *f* and accentuate it definitively on *"umée,"* while approaching slightly from below the note F on which the syllable *"fu"* is sung. That's it. The slight *crescendo* on *"Et sa poussière heureuse"* conveys the idea of feverish desire; the sudden sluggishness of sound on *"reste"* expresses a sort of voluptuousness caused by the exhalation of an aroma that we breathe in with delight; the slow and soft renewal of sound on *"parfumée"* gives a sense of well-being and quietude. To this, one must of course add facial expression, conveying the meaning and tension of the word.

Puis — que par la bles-sure ou-ver — te de mon

cœur— Tu t'écoules de mê — me, ô cé-les-te li-

-queur Inexprimable amour qui m'enflammait pour el — le!

To this point, our singing has been restrained, so to speak; it has only suggested some metaphors, developed some images. Now emotion must come forward and, little by little, achieve dominion; our voice must become more ringing, our stresses more intense. As for our breathing, here are some thoughts: There are different ways of breathing in these first three verses; each has its advantages and disadvantages. My way, no doubt, can be challenged, as can the others; but I have chosen it, therefore I prefer it. I think that we must sing without breathing:

> *Puisque par la blessure ouverte de mon coeur*
> *Tu t'écoules de même,*

with just a short pause in the sound *without a breath* after "*coeur*"; before "*ô céleste liqueur,*" a deep, rapid breath, clearly audible, strongly accentuated—a breath, so to speak, with the quality of a convulsive sigh or a tender sob. Why? Because I am determined to avoid a breath before "*Inexprimable amour*" (although the meaning suggests and even demands one), for I believe that by proceeding in this way, we gain a rather expressive and gripping effect.

Follow me attentively. "*Tu t'écoules de même,* (breath) *ô céleste liqueur, Inexprimable amour qui m'enflammait pour elle!*" After the panting breath that I have indicated, I will make a *crescendo* on "*ô céleste liqueur*" by strongly hissing the *c* and the *s* of "*céleste,*" by doubling the *l* of "*liqueur,*" by pronouncing very clearly the two *i*'s of "*Inexprimable*" without the slightest admixture of another vowel—genuine, raw *i*'s, with jaws closed and the corners of the lips pulled gently back. From "*amour*" onward, the sound should be a *diminuendo,* with a particularly warm note E on "*enflammait,*" coupled with a sort of internal yawn. But in order to give the feeling that this last verse is eventful, one can, even without a breath, interrupt the sound after "*liqueur*" and, before the *i* of "*Inexprimable,*" very lightly give the impression of a sudden stroke of the glottis (all this, of course, rapidly, nimbly, almost imperceptibly). This way of proceeding is difficult, I know, even very difficult. And for that very reason, it is interesting.

What follows is not particularly complicated, at least insofar as it concerns breathing.

Qu'il lui soit par‿don‿né ___ Que mon
mal soit bé‿ni ___ Par de là l'heure humai . ne et le
temps in‿fi‿ni ___ Mon cœur est em‿bau ‿
. mé ___ d'une odeur immor‿tel . le! ___

I really wish I could eliminate this last breath, but it is almost impossible. I cannot accept a breath taken during the final verse although I have often seen it done; but unless one has truly exceptional reserves of air, one cannot sing the last two verses without taking a breath. I manage this feat by being extremely economical with my release of air, but this requires a particularly favorable physiological state and can create some anxiety in the audience. Therefore I take a firm and deep breath after *"infini"* in order to perform the whole at a stretch, broadly and without showing the slightest effort:

Mon coeur est embaumé d'une odeur immortelle!

I sing without nuances, strongly emphasizing the two *m*'s of *"immortelle,"* pronouncing them as if there were three. Despite the face that it seems somewhat arbitrary to sustain a mute *e* during a dotted half-note as indicated by the composer, the note E will be sustained to the end while particular care is taken to pronounce that mute *e* in slightly open manner and not as if it were *leu*. This final verse, sung thus, in a single, powerful melodic stream, should majestically crown and counter with the same sort of radiant stoicism the sorrowful, proud assertion that emerges from this admirable composition.

I mentioned a moment ago that the listener should not be aware of our breathing as we sing. There are, however, exceptions, and these are numerous. Indeed, breathing should frequently be heard, as it can add considerable charm and expressive strength, especially in dramatic music where quick, clearly audible breaths can suggest an anguished gasp, a deep sigh, and so forth. Even in vocal chamber music, in intimate music, such an effect is sometimes necessary. Although more discretion is required here than in the theater (where all effects must conform to the grand scale of the hall or the sets), the breath must be distinct in order to be effective. Quite often, a breath taken when one least expects it can create a delightful, impressive effect, can make a remarkably striking impression.

When Mme Krauss sang Gounod's beautiful oratorio *Gallia* for the first time, she had stage fright, which, among other bothersome effects, makes us breathe badly. Mme Krauss had to sing this well-known, noble phrase:

En _ tends, entends un Dieu sauveur! Tends-
lui les bras rends-lui ton cœur, re _ viens, reviens vers
le Seigneur! le _____ Seigneur Dieu!

During rehearsals, she had taken a breath before "*le Seigneur Dieu!*" However, while she was singing, she had a sudden

inspiration—a not uncommon occurrence in her singing life—
which was to avoid a breath at that particular place in order to
bring the phrase to life on the note F of "*le.*" But scarcely had she
sung that note when she feared she would not have enough breath
for the end of the phrase and would thus be incapable of giving the
final C ("*Dieu*") the necessary fullness and strength. A second
inspiration revealed the perfect solution. Instead of saving that
breath which was likely to give out anyway, she used it up entirely
on "*Seigneur*"; then, after drawing another deep breath, she sang
the word "*Dieu,*" with heartfelt emotion, in splendid isolation. M.
Massenet, who related this anecdote to me, acknowledged that the
effect was overwhelming.

Here is another example of the interpretive resources derived
from the ability to breathe with art, discernment and originality: I
was in Monte Carlo and eagerly looked forward to a performance of *Lohengrin* to be sung by M. Jean de Reszke. My
pleasure turned out to be even greater than anticipated; as soon as
M. de Reszke appeared onstage, I realized he was suffering from a
slight hoarseness and was generally not in top form.

All the same, M. de Reszke is not one of those singers prone to
canceling performances the moment their voice is not in absolutely perfect condition; the merest threat of a cold, the slightest
hoarseness, the most minor discomfort will lead them to decide at
five or six in the evening that they cannot sing; and if they have,
rightly or wrongly, an effect on box-office receipts, you can
imagine the consequences of such a decision. But this is the least of
their concerns: The disarray into which they plunge the opera
house, the disappointment they cause the public and, particularly,
the lack of respect they show the composer, all these leave them
indifferent. But these so-called artists, with rare exceptions, are
not true artists. True artists are infinitely simpler and more
conscientious. Moreover, a true artist is in full possession of his
art, and momentary indispositions do not present such obstacles
that he must refuse to appear in public.

Mme Lilli Lehmann has remarked that except in the case of genuine illness, she has never had to cancel an appearance, either on the eve of the performance or on the day itself. When, in the morning, she finds she is hoarse or otherwise indisposed vocally, she responds to this unpleasant development, not with stolid silence, as many singers do, but with sensible exercises prudently and methodically performed. Mme Lehmann is an extremely wise singer, and one cannot expect everyone to follow her example in similar circumstances; but there are other ways to avoid canceling at the last moment. Rest and will power are in most cases adequate remedies, as most indispositions are not serious.

How frequently one sees a young *chanteuse,* intoxicated by exaggerated successes, taking the liberty of jeopardizing whatever she has achieved by canceling on a whim, because she feels a little tired or because she has *le cafard,* a case of the blues. The *cafard* sometimes lasts a day, sometimes a half-hour; one unpleasant fitting is enough to bring on this morbid state of mind which prevents the singer from lending her support to a musician and a work to which she has pledged herself. For many other reasons (sentimental ones, for example, in which sentiment plays but a small part), singers may fail to function at their best. Once again, true artists, those who see their art as more than a means to gain popular acclaim, do not act in this fashion.

I return to *Lohengrin.* As M. Jean de Reszke sang his first notes, I realized he was suffering from tracheitis, which would deprive him of breath. The moment he began to sing, when he heard his voice in the vast, enclosed spaces of that stage and hall, he realized he would have to struggle throughout the evening against the handicaps of his vocal condition—yet, somehow, his performance was even more beautiful than it would have been without his slight indisposition. Modifying everything he had always done in the role of Lohengrin, breathing in places where he ordinarily did not, but taking care to do so between this or that perfectly appropriate word, his singing became more expressive and appealing than ever before. Not only did his verbal interpretation improve noticeably as a result of his indisposition, but since M. Jean de Reszke is a remarkable artist, he was able to mold his acting, his gestures, his movements, to the new contours of his ravishing singing. Everyone in the theater was under his spell, but very few perceived the special effort involved. It gave me extraordinary pleasure to observe how this admirable singer, with the vigor of the true artist, concealed his discomfort behind the beauty of an original interpretation.

Earlier in this lecture, I sang for you "Le Parfum impérissable." You could see that the breaths in this piece are sometimes quite short and sometimes extremely long—so long that considerable practical experience in the art of breathing is necessary in order to succeed with them. Having to breathe in such varied ways makes the performance of this piece particularly tiring for the singer. The muscles of the breathing apparatus tire much less when they function in a consistent manner than when they are forced to operate in an irregular and jarring fashion.

In the *mélodie* by Gounod that I shall now sing for you, most of the phrases are long. The functioning of the lungs, of the bronchia and the ribs, requires continual tension; but the breaths are almost all of the same length and, once under way at a normal and steady pace, breathing becomes automatic so to speak, without requiring any particular signals from the singer. In this *mélodie*, "Au Rossignol"—one of the most beautiful composed by Gounod—there is only one truly difficult breath; this occurs at the very beginning of the composition:

> *Quand ta voix céleste prélude*
> *Au silence des belles nuits.*

On this subject, permit me yet another word. I have already mentioned that there is, between the singer and the public, a tacit agreement which may never have been formulated up to the present, but which has been accepted without our attempting to analyze it, without our knowing exactly how it was established, unless it arose from a vague sense of indulgence toward the singer who performs an arduous task. It is accepted in singing that breathing may not always occur where logic and good sense dictate. If, in the course of conversation, a person interrupted the phrase to breathe at certain points, the listener would register surprise. But a listening audience has no such reaction if a singer breathes at those same points during a performance; the very fact that the phrase is sung draws the audience into a special complicity with the singer, which prevents the audience from showing surprise at these liberties taken with ordinary breathing patterns.

On one hand, the arbitrary attitude of the singer, and the tolerance of the listening audience, somehow establish certain *conventions;* it is impossible to study and describe them all since there are far too many. However, there is one for which I think I can state the rule; this is the one I mentioned during our analysis of "Le Parfum impérissable," the one which I believe may never before have been formulated. The rule is as follows: *One may, in the course of a phrase, breathe between the subject and the verb, but not between the verb and its object.*

The verb, followed by a pause, however short, is likely to give the impression of a completed statement; and the object, coming after a breath, seems at first to be the subject of a new statement, thus rendering incomprehensible for a second or two the true meaning of the phrase. There are countless examples; but since we were speaking of a certain *mélodie* by Gounod, let us continue with this example. We sing:

Quand ta voix céleste prélude
Au silence des belles nuits.

According to our rule, one can breathe after *"céleste,"* singing: *"Quand ta voix céleste | prélude Au silence des belles nuits."* It is not excellent, it is not logical, but, once again, it is one of those breaths we readily allow in singing, and the ear is so used to such a liberty and to still greater ones that we feel not the slightest shock. All the same, in my opinion it is preferable to breathe only after the two complete lines. But since the music is slow, this creates significant tension in the breathing. Further, I have not taken into consideration that there are many consonants in those two lines: s's, p's, b's, consonants which are essentially "exhalatious," meaning that much breath is exhaled when one pronounces the phrase. Consequently, attention and determination are needed to reach the end of the phrase without showing fatigue or breathlessness. Nevertheless, it is far better not to breathe during that phrase, not only because this is more logical, not only because, in this way, the musical phrase unfolds more naturally, but especially because by avoiding a breath, one lends beauty to the suggested image. By not interjecting a breath, by not interrupting the development of the overarching verbal and musical line, one evokes the star-spangled night in its serene quietude, and the song of the nightingale rises to the sky.

---

[1] [Pierre Garat, celebrated French tenor (1762–1823).]

[2] The aria "Ah, Perfido!"

[3] Lilli Lehmann: *Meine Gesangskunst* (English translation, *How to Sing,* 1902; reprinted 1949).

[4] [Jean-Baptiste Fauré (1830–1914), well-known French baritone.]

Jean de Reszke, Polish tenor (1850–1925), as Roméo in Gounod's *Roméo et Juliette*. Courtesy Andrew Farkas.

III

How to Enunciate in Singing

Mesdames, Mesdemoiselles, Messieurs,

I wish to conjure up in your minds a ventriloquist. A man holds a large doll on his knees and converses with it cheerfully. He asks questions, the doll "answers," but all the while it is the man who speaks, for he has two voices: one from the larynx, the other from the abdomen. It is very amusing, very curious. But it is regrettable that, while failing to attain the perfection of certain music-hall artists (a perfection of skill requiring the same perseverance demanded of the singer), many singers employ in their performances methods that should belong exclusively to the world of the ventriloquist. These singers possess both a speaking voice and a singing voice. Nothing could be more absurd.

Such a person, when invited to sing, apologizes, refuses, yet ends up accepting; but before he begins, he offers a few remarks about his voice or his view of singing—all this in the most natural way possible. Then, suddenly, one hears a sound and wonders where it came from; the voice that has just spoken can no longer be recognized. One has the impulse to look under the furniture, but no! It is indeed the same person who is now singing.

At the same time, two distinct phenomena occur. First, it appears that the voice is coming from elsewhere, from afar, that we are hearing it through something standing between it and us. Second, we perceive in this voice an accent that is faintly human, but it is as if we were listening to the speech of an automaton. The voice strives to make the accent genuine, but it is not; it is a mere echo of a genuine accent. The voice may be lovely, yet it has a quality that is artificial, an enameled, sterilized surface that inspires fear. It is as though a bright, resonant veil hung between the uttered words and the audience; this veil, this transparent, limpid obstacle, is the voice, the singing voice that has come to interpose itself between what the singer is saying and the ear of his listeners. Though the singer may have talent, or at least some degree of ability, he arouses no feelings whatsoever, for there is no point of contact between his words and our ear.

If, while "enunciating," while preserving the rhythm and the style he prefers, he could rid himself of that artificial voice, that vocal affectation, his singing could be quite beautiful. With this small modification to his vocal approach, his singing could become moving, affecting; but whatever it is that intervenes between his words and his audience undermines any sense of reality, thwarts, extinguishes, any expressiveness. It is, as in the Michelangelo ceiling, the tiny distance that separates the finger of God from the finger of man whom He has created. That tiny distance is nothing, yet it is everything.

The *Journal des Goncourt* tells the following tale. The collector Burty, strolling one day along the quays, came upon a lovely drawing signed "Ingres." He bought it and went immediately to Ingres's home. "Look, Master, what I have just bought!" Ingres looked at the drawing and exclaimed: "What? You really believed that this drawing is mine? This drawing is not bad, but do you think I would have drawn an arm like that?" He picked up a pencil. "A knee like this? A shoulder?" As he talked, he made the slightest changes, corrected by a millimeter or two, altered with the merest hint of a line, the contours to which he pointed. And, as he proceeded with these changes—making a sort of tracing barely different from the drawing itself—the drawing came alive, took on an extraordinary reality.

It is the same infinitesimal difference that separates singing that is "sung" and the same singing, with the same intentions and the same style, assimilated to what I shall call, following the lead of M. Jean de Reszke, the "spoken voice"—the voice of the true singer.

It is true that some vocal music cannot be adapted to the "spoken" voice. However, most of the time, the spoken voice is preferable to the other. Indeed, in opera, a singer who uses it immediately distinguishes himself from his colleagues; he attracts attention because he gives the impression of singing *naturally*, while his colleagues do not. Naturalness of timbre is the most important attribute of a singer's diction.

I know only one way to give the impression of singing naturally, and that is to be natural—to place no strain on the vocal apparatus, to take care not to distort its functioning by habitually assuming a precise, unvarying position, which has the double disadvantage of producing tightness and giving everything we sing the same, uniform quality.

First and foremost, in matters of singing, one must guard against all "habits." Singing must be an instrument that lends itself to the expression of all sentiments, of all thoughts; therefore, it must, above all, remain neutral, flexible, passive, yielding to all the caprices of the singer's mind. And yet, rather than searching for ways to give singing that easy mobility, some teachers make it quite impossible by inflicting upon their students a body of arbitrary, invariable rules, often so eccentric that they offend and degrade the laws of nature. What can one say, for example, in favor of this excerpt from a method book whose author I prefer not to identify:

> The best position for a singer is this: the chest inclined slightly forward, the shoulders energetically pushed towards the ground, the posterior thrust backward (a little in the case of men and more so in the case of women), the legs slightly apart so that the lower abdomen, well released, will not return to its original position under the pressure of the thighs. The singer must absolutely avoid curving the back, as this is not only disastrous for the lower back, but flattens the figure (especially in front) and tightens the organs in the abdominal region.

As for the lips, the lady suggests giving them the form of a "spout."

Mesdemoiselles, sometime when you have nothing else to do, try to take the position suggested by Mme L. You may well succeed in devising a pleasing posture, a feat at which I admit I have failed.

Yet I confess to some reluctance to ridicule this distinguished teacher's method, for she goes on to declare that the posture and movements she has recommended, "when performed with precision, will develop the chest, expand it, lower the most elevated shoulders, straighten the back, trim the waist, eliminate the belly no matter how protuberant; it will beautify women and girls by giving their bodies harmonious proportions, and will oblige students"—all students without exception, she assures us—"to let out the upper part of their clothing by fifteen to seventeen centimeters, to take in the back section, lengthen the front section, and reduce the waistline." These improvements, she tells us, these changes, will take place within three or four months; "I have obtained them even in *forty-year-old mothers.*"

I am not certain, after reading all this, that the means suggested are beneficial for singing; but I can see that they impart physical beauty to those who lack it. Thus it would seem appropriate to include this work in whatever collections constitute the libraries of beauty schools and to eliminate it from libraries that have to do with music.

To develop the singing ability of their students, many teachers employ techniques that I would describe as "athletic." I do not deny the usefulness, in some cases, of indicating a desirable position by a slight pressure of the finger upon this or that part of the chest or face. But what can I say of the teacher—now deceased; I knew him well, he was the soul of a gentleman—who would have his students lie on the floor, then place several volumes of the *Larousse Encyclopedia* on their stomachs and sit forcefully upon them, causing the victims to shriek with pain. Following this exercise, he would stand up and announce triumphantly: "You see, you *do* have a B-flat! The only question is how to get it out." A delightful artist, the late Mme Sibyl Sanderson, first described this technique to me, and many others have since confirmed it.

But let us return to diction, and, since I have the good fortune to be able to quote a few lines from Gounod on this subject, I shall let this master speak. (You should know, by the way, that he himself sang very well.)

> Articulation is the external and suggestive form of the word; pronunciation is its internal and intelligible form. The ear perceives the articulated word, while the mind perceives the pronounced word. It is thus easy to under-

stand how carelessness in matters of pronunciation can rob a musical phrase of expression and, consequently, of interest. In a word, articulation is the skeleton and body of the spoken word; but pronunciation constitutes its soul and life.

Let us borrow Gounod's meaning with respect to pronunciation, but let us call it *diction*.

Diction is, so to speak, the esthetic of articulation. It is the overriding concern, the supreme control that orders, balances, embellishes the several mechanisms of elocution. It is through diction that one confers variety and expression to discourse.

Diction consists in many things, of which I shall enumerate only the most important. It consists in greater or lesser rapidity, in the proper spacing of words, parts of phrases or entire phrases; it is diction that punctuates, that stamps the voice with nuances of strength or sweetness, that gives the sound and movement of the voice its faint or forceful gradations. Diction is to the word what the glance, the expression, is to the eye; it gives life to spoken discourse, it injects ideas and feeling into the structure of speech itself. And there you have precisely that quality which a great many singers lack—singers who, heaven knows, sing well, or at least not badly. Their voice is in place, they pronounce correctly, they articulate, but they don't "speak," and therefore they say nothing.

Actually, I was wrong in saying that these singers sang well; they sing well, strictly speaking; their singing is correct in vocal terms. But they do not sing well insofar as their voice does not perform an artistic function. The voice is detached from the word, it remains apart, operating in parallel; it is not suffused with the word, it does not collaborate with it. And I add that by a curious and quite elegant mystery, such singing lacks that supreme beauty of sound which consists precisely of nuance and variety, because not being animated by the word, not being guided, subordinated, controlled by the word, this singing is monotonous. It is monochromatic, whether clear or somber, brilliant or dull; it does not take on different hues, it does not pass through that succession of colorations or shadings without which singing is a dead thing. On the other hand, when these colorations appear, the song is like a streamlet that takes on different tints as it passes under different segments of sky. Its course is even, broken only in a soft, balanced way by a pebble, a slope of the stream-bed, a patch of floating grasses or reeds; it flows along, indolent and even, but its color assumes the most diverse aspects, reflecting now pink, now grey or white clouds or great expanses of blue. Thus singing, in its course and motion, must reflect all the colors of the soul.

When we pronounce a phrase or a succession of phrases, we may remain in the same spiritual state, for generally our frame of mind, our mood, does not change with extreme rapidity. But the harmonics, the vibrations, of each spiritual state are infinite. It is a bad actor who changes his facial expression with every word of a phrase; but still worse is the one who recites a long passage in a monotone, giving the words none of the inflections, the slight but all-important nuances, required by the fluctuations of thought and feeling.

Therefore, genuinely convincing diction originates in the heart and mind of the singer. But, as I have already noted, art is not the same as ethics, where intention is as good as fact. In diction, the most admirable intentions are useless if they are not adequately carried out by the vocal apparatus.

Now, as I have said, we make a serious mistake when we separate diction from singing itself. When one hears about a singer: "He sings so well! What a pity that one cannot understand what he says!" be assured that, far from singing "so well," this singer sings very badly. Singing and diction are inseparable, and this is the idea I will seek to demonstrate today.

When we sing, no matter how natural and effortless our singing, our vocal organs do not remain in a single position, as they do when we speak. This shifting of position has several causes.

First, the singing voice obeys the music; therefore, it does not remain, as does the speaking voice, within more or less the same register. Rather, it moves upward and downward, and the larynx must perform these motions with absolute exactitude and obedience. When we sing, moreover, we must project the sound further than when we are speaking in a normal way. There are many other reasons for the shifting positions of our vocal organs, but among these, the most important is this: As we sing, we pronounce words, and these words are made up of vowels and consonants. Now, vowels and consonants have a very definite influence on the quality and color of the sound. If, when singing, we pronounce the vowels exactly as we do when speaking, our singing voice becomes jerky and irregular, and the sound loses all homogeneity: This note is resonant, the next is muffled; some are guttural, others are nasal and so on. If we wish our voice to remain even and smooth, to undergo only those modulations we choose to impose for the sake of nuance and inflection, we must forcibly transform the vowels (especially the vowels) and the consonants in ways that will compensate for the effect on the sound caused by the shifting positions of the larynx.

I offer this example to make my meaning clear. You perhaps know the short, delightful aria "Ombre heureuse" ("Blessed Spirit") in Gluck's *Orphée*.[1] In interpreting this piece, an absolute evenness of sound, a total vocal quietude, is necessary to evoke the peace and enchantment of the Elysian sojourn. Now there is, in the third bar of this aria, a rather notable challenge for the soprano voice, which, as you know, does not lend itself well to the pronunciation of words set in the high register, particularly words with closed vowels and strong consonants.

Cet a - si - le ai - mable et tran -
-quil - le par le bon-heur - est ha - bi - té —

The word *"habité"* set upon these high notes is the most difficult to articulate with the necessary softness. In a laudable effort to pronounce well, less skillful singers will struggle painfully on those two A notes, enunciating the *i* and the *e* purely, the *b* and *t* correctly—but with a voice that is choking, with a shrill and shabby sound. Other singers, preoccupied solely with vocal quality, do not hesitate to enunciate thus:

which is awful. However, by adding a little *u* to the *i* and a little *eu* to the *e,* the singer may succeed in giving the impression of a perfect pronunciation while, at the same time, protecting the fullness of the sound.

I am dealing with rather elementary matters in order to make my point quickly. But I hope I have made it clear that when we speak of diction, we must also concern ourselves with the vocal mechanism and with articulation, since, in matters of singing, all is linked and intermingled.

As for articulation, there is so much I might tell you that I hardly know where to begin. Further, I ask myself whether this is the time and place to undertake a study of phonetics. Consider for a moment: We should have to examine one after the other the various foreign and provincial accents, faults of pronunciation such as lisping, mispronouncing the letter *l,* and especially the guttural or exaggerated rolling of the uvular *r.* The latter practice is more common than the others, although one could not claim to sing and gutturalize the *r* at the same time, despite the examples of the great Elleviou, who created the role of Joseph in Egypt,[2] or the brilliant Schroeder-Devrient, who is said to have gutturalized abominably.

So, in light of its vastness, let us not linger on the subject of articulation. All the same, I would like to note that it is by no means necessary to grimace with your mouth in order to articulate well. Furthermore, nothing is more disastrous to correct tone production. Any contortion of the vocal apparatus influences the process by which sound takes wing and consequently inflicts distortion. In addition, grimaces are distracting, and the audience soon stops listening, to watch with a certain anguish mixed with disgust the facial performances of the singer. Yet I, as I stand before you, am well aware that when I sing, I knit my brows, I lift them, I close my left eye slightly and have a tendency to lean my head backwards, which is very bad since it adds an affectation to my attitude. I know all this, and when I think about it, I try to correct myself, though I do not always succeed.

Still, after drawing to your attention the ridiculous mannerisms with which I am afflicted, I am going to pay myself a compliment. It is only fair, don't you agree? My friends are often astonished that I can sing with a cigarette, which I am actually smoking, between my lips. Do not think that I boast of this ability as if it were something worthy of admiration. If I sing with a cigarette in my mouth, it is because, unfortunately, I am a chain smoker, and the cigarette has become a part of myself. But if I can keep it in my mouth without dropping it, it is because I barely move my lips while singing, and this is the compliment I pay myself. In order to articulate clearly, it is not necessary to move the lips constantly and to inflict strange shapes upon one's mouth. First, this gives a jerky quality to the singing; but more than that, when one has many words to pronounce in a short period of time, the spectacle becomes grotesque.

To produce, to form, a sound, the singer must perform three different actions simultaneously: Place the larynx in a certain position, at a certain height; project the sound; and support it, which is to say, color it, guide it, and modify it according to the infinitely varied requirements of the words and music.

Here we touch on the delicate and perplexing question of the different vocal registers. How many registers do we have? We can't expect to find the answer in treatises on singing methods, because they diverge widely on this point.

The word *register* refers to a series of notes that can be sung easily, without the necessity of changing the position of the larynx. For example, we usually identify three registers in the female voice: the chest register, the mixed register, and the high register which is called the "head voice." The quality which indicates the end of one register and the beginning of the next is an appreciable change in timbre; in women's voices, this is particularly noticeable at the juncture between the "chest voice" and the "mixed voice"; frequently, at this point, we hear a sort of break which the Italians call *distacco.* You have all heard *Faust,* and you know that the artist who sings the role of Dame Marthe Schwertlein always performs a sort of involuntary Tyrolese yodel when she says to Mephistopheles:

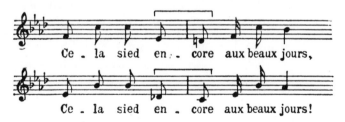

Ce . la sied en . core aux beaux jours,

Ce . la sied en . core aux beaux jours!

In the male voice, the register differences are less obvious. But let us not become entangled in questions which could lead us astray. To give an idea of the diversity of opinions, we should note only that Garcia and many others agree on three different registers. Fauré and a few others say there are only two; at least one method I have read holds that there are five.

I am hesitant to offer my personal opinion on this question; however, since it is corroborated by Mme Lilli Lehmann, why not? I believe, as she does, that in truth there is no such thing as different vocal registers. If there are some singers or voice teachers in the audience whom these ideas offend, I beg their pardon; but it seems to me that since each note, each sound, requires a different position of all the organs, from the depth of the lungs and the diaphragm up to the muscles of the forehead—following the labyrinthine path of the sound—it is impossible to assign an exact place, and always the same place, to a particular group of notes.

Once the larynx is set, we must produce the sound. How do we produce the sound? It is generally agreed that there are two ways to do so. The second—about which I speak first since it is less controversial than the first—the second consists in emitting the sound only after the exhalation of breath has begun. Many teachers object to this approach, because it is imprecise, because it does not produce a clear sound and because it tends to waste breath.

The other method of sound production is the stroke of the glottis. Ah, the stroke of the glottis! What a lot of talk it has provoked! Its most illustrious advocate is M. Fauré.[3]

But does anyone really know what a stroke of the glottis is? It is something very difficult to explain, and M. Fauré himself provides a definition that is far from clear. Yet is is very easy to perform. M. Fauré has never tired of advocating the stroke of the glottis. He extols its merits and asserts that the glottal jolt is our only hope of salvation. Mme Lilli Lehmann, without specifically referring to the stroke of the glottis, implicitly recommends it in her descriptions of the proper approach to sound production. Mme Viardot, in the brief instructions that precede her exercises for the female voice, breathes not a word about the glottal stroke; she seems unaware of its existence. Massenet considers the stroke of the glottis a crime against heaven, while Crosti is indifferent. M. Victor Maurel is firmly opposed to the stroke of the glottis, and anyone who has heard this eminent artist knows it. Verdhurt blasts the poor stroke of the glottis without pity, and so on.

One of the fiercest adversaries of the glottal stroke is Paul Marcel, who has written an interesting and amusing book on singing. The idea that one might produce these glottal jolts arouses his indignation to the point where I believe he would call death down on the heads of those who dared to recommend it. The following phrase appears in his little book: "I have before me a treatise by one of our great masters of singing, who recommends the glottal attack but who, when he himself sings, does his best to avoid this practice."

Marcel is speaking of M. Fauré, contending that this master has never used the stroke of the glottis. A bit later, Marcel says: "I repeat, M. Fauré has always attacked the tone with a great deal of clarity and has always sung very accurately without ever having recourse to the glottal stroke."

I believe we have a misunderstanding here. I do not think M. Fauré ever intended to suggest that a stroke of the glottis is necessary at every note; one would thus ascribe to this incomparable singer an absurd idea that he certainly did not entertain. M. Fauré evidently recommends the stroke of the glottis for the attack on the first sound, in other words, after one breath has been completed and as a new series of sounds begins.

Ombre chè - re,   om - bre venge - res - se.

He finds that this method facilitates the placement of the voice and the projection of the timbre in a clear and precise way, and that is all. Those among you who would like to experiment should attempt the stroke of the glottis while pronouncing a consonant. This will suffice to demonstrate that the feat is extremely difficult, if not impossible, which in turn proves that if M. Fauré recommended the frequent use of the glottal attack, it was only in the course of exercises, in training, in order to provide a good foundation for the basic source of sound, but not in performance where tone production must always be governed by thought and feeling.

I was recently told that M. Fauré used a glottal stroke frequently—not at every note, as some obscure rivals pretend to believe, but, in truth, quite frequently—and sometimes at odd moments. In *Hamlet,*[4] for example, he sang, instead of *"Ma mère,"* *"Ma m-ère,"* using a stroke of the glottis between the *m* and the *è*. No doubt this enhanced the resonance of the sound and projected the note further, with more impact; yet I find it difficult, despite my immense respect for this admirable singer, to approve, in principle, the use of the glottal stroke on a consonant. This is the kind of technique which, when performed by others (for M. Fauré was marvelously able to control it), risks becoming unbearable.

Nonetheless, it seems to me that the glottal stroke, used at the outset of certain phrases beginning with a vowel, as, for example: *"Amour, que veux-tu de moi?"* ("Love, what do you want of me?") or *"Ah, si la liberté me doit être ravie!"* ("Ah, if my liberty must be taken away!") can be quite beneficial. On the other hand, in other phrases beginning with a vowel, such as: *"O nuit divine, je t'implore"* ("Oh divine night, I implore you"), it would be improper, as it would give the first sound of the phrase a precision that would alter the airy sweetness the text and music require.

Here, since I have mentioned in passing the aria from *Amadis* by Lully, let me sing it for you. It is one of the most beautiful and moving creations of the great Florentine of Versailles, and it also demonstrates a few uses of the glottal stroke. The aria is sung by Arcabonne, the mischievous magician, whose heart, up to now, has never known love. For the first time, she experiences this burst of tender feeling, and the sentiment, so new to her, is not merely troubling but annoying. The emotions it arouses are so foreign that they become a form of suffering, and she rises up with a start, as if responding to a physical attack, to sing:

From the beginning, great energy is required; one must seize the musical phrase and hold it fast, as in a hand-to-hand fight, right up to the words *"de moi."* And in this case, one can appreciate how very useful the stroke of the glottis will be on the *A* of *"Amour"*— a true stroke of the glottis, almost harsh, that strikes, seizes, the note.

I would not add a clear stroke of the glottis on *"Non, ne t'oppose point"* ("Non, do not be opposed"); but I would use one that was only slightly marked and preceded by a strong exhalation of breath: a double diminution of tension that gives a mournful yet firm accent to this exclamation. A similar stroke of the glottis is necessary on *"haine"* ("hatred"); but here, the release of breath is less marked, while the stroke of the glottis is emphasized sharply (*h* <| *aine*).

But Arcabonne is weakening. In the line, *"Je ne veux inspirer que l'horreur et l'effroi"* ("I would inspire only horror and fright"), and even before, when she sings: *"Non, ne t'oppose point au penchant qui m'entraine!"* ("No, do not oppose the direction I must take!"), there is, so to speak, a retreat; it seems she has a presentiment of love's inevitable victory, and it is imperiously, almost convincingly, that she now says: *"Amour, que veux-tu de moi?"* ("Love, what do you want of me?") Still, she is resisting, so this second *"Amour"* must be uttered with a certain nervous concentration. Here the stroke of the glottis should be totally different from that at the beginning; but there must be one, at all costs.

Let us continue:

Mon coeur aurait trop de peine
A suivre une douce loi.

My heart is too hard, too stubborn,
To obey a tender law.

Here she is almost speaking to herself, as I perceive it. I also feel that sorrow, even despair and tears, are appropriate to:

C'est mon sort d'être inhumaine.

It is my fate to be inhuman.

And so, since Arcabonne is now vanquished, her strength annihilated, since she has succumbed to tenderness along with shame, I would avoid the slightest glottal stroke on the third and last *"Amour,"* which I would link without breathing to *"inhumaine."* I would breathe after *"Amour,"* with a sort of anguished aspiration, making particularly audible the scraping of the air against the sides of the larynx, and I would sing the rest of the song sorrowfully, as if suppressing deep sobs.

Since we have already spoken of M. Fauré, permit me to make a slight digression in order to add a few more observations about him. To speak of a man like M. Fauré, to evoke his personality, merely to pronounce his name, is to speak about singing, to fill the spirit with thoughts of singing.

I must tell you, Mesdemoiselles, that I have a good memory for sounds. This one must have in order to sing, as some people have a memory for faces, as painters recall contours and colors. The great surgeon Trousseau, towards the end of his life, still distinctly remembered the patients he had tended at the hospital as an intern, the details of their injuries, the various forms of ill health he had seen among them[5]—a marvelous repertory of references, a mental card-index always at his disposal.

Frontispiece of the libretto by Quinault for *Amadis,* opera by J.-B. Lully. Design by Jean I. Berain, 1684.

Overleaf. Arcabonne's aria from Act II of Lully's *Amadis.* Reproduced from *Les Plus Beaux Airs de l'Opéra François,* Vol. I. J. & W. Chester Ltd., London, 1926.

I
AMADIS
(AIR d'ARCABONNE)

Lully
rév. par Gabriel Grovlez

Allegro moderato

PIANO

A - mour, que veux - tu de moi? Mon cœur n'est pas fait pour toi. Mon

cœur n'est pas fait pour toi. Non, ne t'op-po - se point au pen-

-chant qui m'en - trai-ne, Je suis ac-coù-tu-mée à res-sen - tir la hai - ne, Je

ne veux ins-pi-rer que l'hor-reur et l'ef-froi. A - mour, que veux-tu de moi? Mon coeur au-rait trop de pei-ne A sui-vre une dou - ce loi C'est mon sort d'è-tre in-hu-mai-ne A mour, que veux tu de moi? Mon coeur n'est pas fait pour toi. Mon coeur n'est pas fait pour toi.

Likewise a singer must build up a repertory of sounds and draw on it perpetually. I have had the great pleasure of hearing M. Fauré sing, when he was already quite old. He sang in the duet from *Mireille*,[6] the arioso from *Le Roi de Lahore*,[7] and the prayer of Dimitri.[8] I remember his voice well; but I must admit that I have no clear recollection of the famous stroke of the glottis, the object of so much discussion and dispute. I do remember, however, that his singing, while extraordinarily *sostenuto* and *legato,* had a certain hammered quality. Perhaps that characteristic was due to repeated glottal strokes.

I was too young then to pay serious attention to the matter. However, by searching my memory, I can recall a few strokes of the glottis in the *Mireille* duet. A few years later, upon learning that M. Fauré occasionally sang at vespers in a certain church, I went to hear him. There, standing behind a pillar, I listened with profound emotion as a voice rose to the very arches, a voice I would not describe as marvelous, but which, to the ear of someone who loves and venerates singing, was supremely impressive. As I listened to M. Fauré, I had the distinct impression that I was observing a remarkable work of marquetry in sound. Each tone, each portion of each tone, was examined, shaped, ornamented and fitted into place in the most surprising fashion. And controlling and managing this sound, animating it, was an effortless, abundant, seemingly endless supply of breath. If the glottal stroke played a role in this singing, well then, I am all for it. Indeed, I must admit, I do not believe that one can sing with no recourse whatsoever to the stroke of the glottis, and even those who profess to avoid it use it. I say this because, quite often, while attempting to perform an extremely smooth emission, a stroke of the glottis must be used, but so lightly that it is imperceptible; the sound then emerges:

> . . . *En éclatant*
> *Tout bas, comme un bouton de rose.*
>
> . . . By opening
> Softly, like the bud of a rose.

I must add that M. Fauré's *Method of Singing*—which is obviously a little like Michelet's *Histoire de France* in that, in order to understand it, one must already know a great many things—is the most captivating book ever written on singing. There is something of a superior, disdainful tone that commands respect; in addition, the style is clear and sure.

But let us draw our conclusions. The sound must emerge naturally, easily, and must reveal no effort whatsoever on the part of the performer. The moment the singing is labored, it is clear that the singer sings badly; and if an expert singer experiences pain or discomfort when performing a passage, it is because he is singing it badly, and he must therefore sing it differently.

And so, one cannot condemn too strongly certain means used by a few teachers—means which are ridiculous, even criminal. One teacher, whose name I shall not reveal but who, a few years ago, was all the rage and incited genuine fanaticism among the students she had collected, used during lessons (and recommended for use during practice sessions) an instrument introduced into the mouth "in order to lift up the uvula and hold it in a forward position." (Some of this teacher's students disclosed to me in confidence that her lessons required less the presence of a piano than that of a basin . . .)

Another published method suggests "that a little stick, rounded at both ends, should be used to enlarge the mouth and pharyngeal cavities, and a flat ruler is useful to dilate and elongate the four pillars of the uvula and those of the larynx by constantly pushing them back towards the soft palate when they resist the restraints of the spatula." This really sounds like something from the memoir of M. Fleurant in *Le Malade Imaginaire*. This instructor perhaps goes a bit too far in claiming that it is impossible to sing without the use of spatulas, rulers or little sticks rounded at both ends, for he implies that before his marvelous inventions, good singers did not exist.

I think that nothing is more muddleheaded and contrary to

artistic purposes than to introduce into the study of singing—
where thought, mental effort and much that is metaphysical must
always preside—clumsy means that debase this noble art and
reduce it to a distasteful physical chore.

But let us return to our technical description. First came the
breath, then the setting of the larynx, then the production of sound
(with or without the stroke of the glottis). Our attention must turn
now to how to sustain that sound. It is here that *"l'appui,"* "the support," plays its part.

Breath support—I mentioned it in my previous lecture, but I
passed over it too hastily, so I repeat it today—breath support is
one of the vital secrets, one of the most essential fundamentals of
singing. Without support, singing is merely an outline, a hazy
indication. You will remember that when I sang "Le Parfum
impérissable" the other day, at a certain moment I stopped supporting the tone, and I explained my reasons for doing so.

Et sa poussière heureuse en res . te parfu . mé . e.___

But such cases are exceptions which may seem charming, but
for a few seconds and no more. Singing, deprived of its support, is
ineffective and, in any case, has no artistic value.

Unfortunately, many singers make no distinction between
supporting and *pushing.* These are two very different things; very
rarely should one push, while greater or lesser support is nearly
always required.

What is support? Support is a distinct contact between breath
and tone, which may be pronounced or barely perceptible but is
always exact and firm. Even in the most tenuous *pianissimo* singing,

one should not, I believe, be aware of the support, yet it must be there. Lacking support, the sound that emerges is flabby, disembodied, drowned in a great sea of breath. A sound without support is like a draft of air coming through a crack: One wants to stop up the crack, to shore up the voice. Moreover, the vowels always seem to be surrounded by a small halo of haze, as if the singer had wrapped them in aspirated *h*'s. Finally, sound without support cannot vary in intensity. Through support, one increases or decreases the power of the sound; without support, these transformations are impossible.

But where does this support take place? Is it at the pit of the stomach? Is it higher, in the larynx? Is it near the lips? Sometimes it is in one place and sometimes in another, depending upon the circumstances.

There is still another form of support, known only to a few. M. Jean de Reszke described it nicely when a singer who was about to sing a few bars of a love song asked him: "How should the voice be supported?"

"With the heart," he replied.

A voice supported "with the heart" has a slightly hushed quality, something private and enclosed, which removes all stridency from the sound and gives it a profound and penetrating quality. But this requires a special gift which is not acquired through work or repetition.

[1] [Note that in 1774, Gluck himself rewrote his *Orfeo* (originally in Italian) to a French text by Moline, for the famous tenor Legros in Paris.]

[2] [*Joseph en Egypte*, an opera by Méhul (1807).]

[3] [Jean-Baptiste Fauré (1830–1914), a famous French baritone.]

[4] [*Hamlet*, an opera by Ambroise Thomas (1868).]

[5] Article written by M. Paul Bourget about Professor Poncet (*Revue hebdomadaire*, October 4 1913).

[6] [*Mireille*, an opera by Gounod (1864).]

[7] [*Le Roi de Lahore*, an opera by Massenet (1877).]

[8] [From Moussorgsky's *Boris Godunov*, 1874. Fauré occasionally sang tenor roles.]

Nellie Melba, Australian soprano (1861–1931), in the title role of Massenet's *Manon*. Courtesy William R. Moran.

IV

What Do We Mean by Having Style?

Mesdames, Mesdemoiselles, Messieurs,

What do we mean by *having style?* This is the subject of today's lecture. Indeed, what *do* we mean by *having style?* In fact, I don't have the faintest idea. Often I hear it said that this or that singer has or does not have style, but I do not understand why.

To begin with, what is style? If I am not mistaken, and without specifying any particular art form, style is the whole of the specific means that an artist uses to communicate his or her thoughts or emotions. But the singer is not his own interpreter, he is the interpreter of the composer, and the number of composers is endless; they represent different epochs, different countries and greatly different musical genres. Now, Voltaire says (and Voltaire is incomparable when it comes to the short, pithy insight): *"The first law is to conform one's style to one's subject."* Accordingly, I cannot imagine that there is a singing style, a definite style, that could apply to the interpretation of all music. It does not seem possible to me to sing in the same way a dramatic scene and a *chanson* by Darcier, an excerpt from Monteverdi and an aria by Grétry, a selection from Mozart and one from Debussy.

However, if a singer sings a Bach aria well, if he or she sings it with the restrained expression that all agree is required in the interpretation of this master, we do not hesitate to say that this singer "has style," even if he or she subsequently sings a song by Schumann very poorly. Why? By what law do we withhold the stamp of stylistic approval from the fanciful, passionate accents which appropriately serve Schumann yet grant it to the restrained tones and bland coloring that is most often suitable for Bach? Would it not be more logical to say: "This person understands the style of Bach and does not understand the style of Schumann," or: "This person sings Baroque music better than Romantic music"? But no, we say instead: "She sang that song by Schumann poorly, but she sang the Bach aria admirably. *At any rate, she has considerable style.*"

Now you know why I cannot understand what is meant by *having style*—or, more precisely, you know why to my mind the word *style* is used incorrectly. We imagine that this word signifies simplicity, accuracy, restraint; and, as always in the case of a simplistic exaggeration, we carry this concept too far, to the point of believing that the more restrained the singing, the greater the style; that the less we indulge in nuances, the nearer we come to style; that the more subdued the expression, the more austere or simply indifferent to ordinary human emotions the singer appears to be (all the while uttering fervent, sorrowful, tender, furious, caressing or passionate words), the more uniform the articulation and restricted the variation in tone quality, in brief, the drier and colder the interpretation, the more "style" the singer possesses.

In espousing this view, we have completely forgotten that the word *style* only implies simplicity, restraint, accuracy, in those works in which accuracy, restraint and simplicity are appropriate to the music, and that in those works where mannerism, affectation, caprice, are in order, it is precisely by means of caprice, affectation and mannerism that one arrives at "style." There is no more merit in knowing how to sing in a simple, straightforward style than in a picaresque or affected style; it is every bit as difficult to interpret the roles of Falstaff, Don Quichotte or Manon as it is to interpret Orpheus, Agamemnon or Alcestis; it is as difficult for a bass to do justice to the aria of the Drum-Major in *Le Caïd* as it is to do justice to the aria in Bach's cantata *God Is My King*.

So many people are mistaken in this matter. They seem to believe that the degree of talent called forth in interpreting so-called classical music is higher and somehow worthier than the degree of talent needed to interpret other kinds of vocal or dramatic performances. Clearly, they have forgotten that Classic composers often brought onstage some quite vulgar and grotesque characters. They *are* part of the Classic repertoire, but singers would be ill-advised to interpret them in the same way as the noble characters of the same repertoire.

All this is most confusing, and it would be presumptuous to hope to sort it out today. Let us be content to note that there are as many styles as there are musical genres, different composers and different compositions.

Thus the chief difficulty for the singer consists in choosing the *right* style. It is for this reason that I persist in believing a singer must have a great deal of general knowledge, not only about singing and the different kinds of vocal music, but also about history and the arts through the successive periods of civilization. A composer, like any other artist, is both a creative force and a reflection of his own time and milieu. Let us consider Gluck, for example (for everyone is more or less familiar with Gluck): It is absolutely necessary to understand that although he wonderfully expressed the emotional qualities of certain characters and wonderfully depicted certain scenes of ancient Greece, he remained a man of the 18th century; his conception of Grecian antiquity was that of a man of his own time. Only with this understanding can we interpret Gluck in his proper "style."

Likewise, to faithfully interpret Lully's music, it is necessary to remember that although he lived, one could even say "reigned," at the court of Louis XIV, whose magnificence and mannered elegance his music constantly reflects, he began life as a cook's apprentice in Florence, and from these humble beginnings, he retained something of a lowbrow mentality; a taste for the burlesque and a fondness for showy display. The singer must bear all this in mind if he or she wishes to truly interpret Lully's works. It should also be noted that Lully untiringly insisted that singers should strive for realistic, human expression. He once remarked to a *cantatrice:* "If you wish to sing my music well, go to hear Mlle Champmeslé."[1] In short, under Lully's ample wig was a mind in a permanent state of excitement, an anxious and feverish brain. Thus it will behoove the singer, while respecting the exterior form of the music in all its stately nobility, to reveal as well the fiery sensibility it conceals.

If you should sing a beautiful Schubert song—"Das Zügenglöcklein," "Der Winterabend" or "Der Wanderer," for example—you must, of course, present the music and the text printed on the pages; but you must do so in a style—a style of pronouncing, singing, expressing oneself in short—that is altogether different from the style one would choose to interpret Lully or Gluck, a style that summons up the era, the atmosphere, of Schubert's life. As I listen to you, my mind must fill with floating images of a Viennese salon, warmly lit by glowing lamps, in which women wearing light-colored gowns and men in tight frock-coats with large cravats over starched shirts devote their whole attention to the soft, expressive singing of a stout young blond man who, with his gold-rimmed spectacles beneath his broad forehead and his cap of curly hair, accompanies himself on the piano. When I listen to a performance of Schumann's "Frauenliebe und -leben," I want to be able, as I share the emotions of this certain "woman," to imagine Schumann himself at any moment, now smiling, his heart suffused with the sweetness of a first love, now haggard and despairing.

Singing is beautiful only when it is poetical, evocative, haunting; only when it succeeds, due to a perfect blend of indefinable allusions, together with what we might call "etymological ramifications," in conveying precise impressions. A true singer can invest meaning in even the arabesques of a vocalise, can put them to the service of an esthetic ideal and use them to evoke a feeling or an image.

Style, then, is the sum total of all the elements to which I have alluded, and not that austerity of approach that so many people wrongly advocate in the interpretation of early music. The moment a work is classified as "early," people of this view will tell you it should be sung formally, with the slightest of nuances, in a cold and modest manner. I have never been able to share this view. At its inception, "early" music was thoroughly modern, and today's music, however "modern" it is now, will one day belong to the past. Will it then be necessary to sing it differently from the way we do today? The day someone ventures to sing *Tristan and Isolde* coldly and circumspectly—since this belongs in the category of "early music"—that day we will be guilty of a piece of ridiculous nonsense. Imagine, too, how silly it would be to "pontificate" in the midst of Don Giovanni's serenade.

The real significance of Gluck, his place in the history of opera, is to be found in the change that he brought to dramatic declamation. Before him, dramatic singing was characterized by a certain polite and solemn tone, which, certainly, attained a high level of honesty on occasion, but which nonetheless fell far short of realism. No matter how passionate, violent or tender the emotions portrayed, they were all given a sort of Versailles style, marked by pomp, heavy elegance and abundant glitter. Rameau brought to dramatic music not only a delightful grace, but a certain liveliness of feeling and other charms that I shall not take the time to delineate here. But it was Gluck, though he was not always successful, who sought to portray fury, supreme, heart-rending sorrow, heroic delusion, the confusion of gesture and accent that reveal inner turmoil. He maintained that, in the process of composing, he drew his inspiration directly from life, from the "spoken" accent upon which, through music, he imposed a purely artistic transformation, a simple act of transposition that kept the basic realism intact. This artistic posture is confirmed by his contemporaries, who wrote that this great dramatist composed his operas by acting out the various roles in his room, while shouting, pulling his hair, falling on his knees, crawling on the floor, reproducing every movement of his characters. And this is the music that some people today would sing calmly, temperately, with the barest trace of emotion, stripping away every shred of excitement, emotion, extravagance? How absurd!

We are told that developing the proper style is difficult for singers; at the same time, all the elements that could complicate the development of style—all traces of passion, emotion, expression, life—are removed from the singing process, thus reducing the stature of the singer himself. At least, if we sing in time, with a minimum of nuance, with moderation and unending simplicity, we can be sure we will commit no grave stylistic errors. The difficulty, the genuine problem, lies in the judicious management of the music *while bringing to the interpretation a significant share, an immense share, a preponderant share, of expression, thought and realism.*

Absurd notions of style have given birth to some quite inept traditions which only serve to distort our interpretations of the old masterpieces. The interpretation of virtually all Gluck's arias suffers from such false stylistic notions. Nuances, variations in timbre and tempi, are chosen by a particular artist, poorly understood and transmitted by a later singer, then inaccurately and carelessly imitated by those who follow, until, in the end, a hard shell of stylistic convention surrounds the living arias, concealing their true beauty and accorded the honorable name of *traditions.*

Ah! traditions; how naïve of us to pay the slightest attention to them. How can we possibly imagine how the singers of the 18th century sang when we have such difficulty discovering how those of only fifty, forty or thirty years ago sang?

M. Fauré is still living. So, one might ask, how was M. Fauré on the stage? I do not have the slightest idea. I have heard a great deal about him and his talent from admirers as well as detractors; yet I cannot conjure up a clear and genuine mental image of M. Fauré's dramatic personality.

But, really, how absurd it is to think that the emotional quality of a great artist can be conveyed to us through the performances of *other* artists! One of our most enduring traditions—and one of the least useful—derives from the interpretation of Orpheus by Mme Viardot.[2] As you may know, Mme Viardot was widely considered to be incomparable in that role, so much so that every singer since has imitated her performances or sought inspiration from her interpretation. However, I am confident that even if it were possible to form a vague idea of Mme Viardot's approach to singing the aria "Che faro senza Euridice," even if we knew that she proceeded by gradually intensifying her display of despair, we would be incapable of discovering exactly *how she did it.* Let us be satisfied with the knowledge that in her interpretation she was, in turn, sobbing, dejected and fierce—and let us profit from that valuable information. In spite of very sketchy evidence, singers today attempt to recreate Mme Viardot's interpretation of this *Orfeo* aria. But their desire to sing with "style" undermines the ideal of projected vehemence, and the results are usually miserable. We end up with a weak counterfeit of her probably sublime performance.

Generally, one sings the scene with a rather academic despair. In the last stanza of the aria, I would like to have a touch of hysteria, a moment of frightful realism, set in stark contrast to the first aria of the first act, in which Orfeo's anguish is expressed by something akin to prostration; when he is near the tomb, surrounded by wailing women, his sense of decorum prevents him from giving full rein to his grief. But in the aria "Che faro," he is standing by the corpse of his beloved, convinced that she is now lost to him forever. In my vision, he falls upon her lifeless body, embraces it, tears at his own face and, in the solitude of the forest, gives himself up completely to the terrifying excesses of immense despair. I believe that any sort of animal outburst, anything resembling the cry of a wounded beast, would be excusable here.

In another opera by Gluck, *Iphigenia in Tauris,* there is a scene where again I would condone near-hysteria. Iphigenia, overwhelmed by the horror of what she has just learned of—the murder of her mother by her own brother, the double assassination that has tarnished the palace of the Atrides, the merciless punishment that awaits her unfortunate brother—seeing herself as alone in the world, exiled, far from her homeland, already growing old (for you must not forget that Iphigenia in Tauris is no longer the young girl from Aulis, but a woman who has suffered, a high priestess of Diana whose particular duties are terrible, atrocious, since she must sacrifice, kill with her own hand, human beings to be offered as oblation to the goddess), has, at this point, reached the depths of suffering and horror and understandably surrenders to utter despair. Surrounded by her young priestesses, she sobs, she screams, she howls. Only a complete lack of taste, knowledge and sincerity, only a ridiculous and tawdry artistic contradiction could allow an artist to sing this frantic music with restraint; this music in which Gluck has expressed, even in the exaggerated, divided disposition of the syllables, a paroxysm of pain, an almost physical rending which, near the end, no doubt approaches the limits of sanity. At this particular moment, I think that Iphigenia loses all self-control, that she is consumed by suffering, that her muscles tighten, her eyes become fixed, that she freezes in a morbid state engendered by grief. Repeatedly, she cries out the same words set on high notes to which Gluck has juxtaposed dissonances that are truly painful, minor seconds that, repeatedly stressed, accented, hammered, seem designed to tear one's heart apart by their frenzied harshness. The whole scene is frightful; the young priestesses, slowly overcome by the depths of Iphigenia's suffering, join her in crying out despair, becoming a chorus of wailers, howlers, around that noble figure.

At such a moment, the interpreter must forget her voice, her breathing, her tone, indeed everything about herself. But since only a singer in full possession of her art should attempt to sing Iphigenia in the first place, such an artist will be able, without risk, to set aside all technical considerations and to give herself entirely to this overwhelming lamentation. If the singer is short of breath, so be it; let her breathe any which way, between words if need be, with hiccups, in jerks; if her voice is muffled or strident, it matters not. All this is appropriate to the sense of boundless grief the singer must project. The more she appears confused, the more she seems beside herself, the better she is able to project Gluck's reality.

I realize that I seem to offer countless variations on the phrase: "To sing this or that, one must remember something or other." Well, in order to remember something, one must have prior knowledge of it. And most of today's singers know nothing. Even if we accept that they know how to sing, which is frequently debatable, they know nothing of what makes singing interesting or moving. The reader may well object that it is not their fault, since they have not been instructed in these matters. But such an objection is wrong-headed; there are many competent teachers who do their best to teach singers at least the rudiments of expressive singing. The Paris Conservatoire has always offered classes in dramatic literature and in the history of music. But voice students never attend these classes, and when we criticize them for this, as I have often done, they find support—notably among the press—among writers, flatterers who leap to their defense.

Two years ago, after a competition at the Conservatoire, I wrote in the *Journal:*

> Most students do not seem to have the faintest notion of the historical or literary relevance of the characters they attempt to incarnate. The Aïdas have never read Maspero [the French Egyptologist, 1846–1916]; the Didos have no idea of Virgil; the Salammbôs [*Salammbô,* an opera by the French composer Reyer, 1823–1909, with a libretto by Flaubert] are much more likely to perceive the heroine through the medium of Mme Caron or Mme Bréval [leading French divas][3] than through Flaubert; interpreters of Henry VIII [in the opera by Saint-Saëns] know nothing of Shakespeare and Holbein; Roméos lack youth, and Juliettes think themselves "ingénues" because they are sopranos.

These harmless lines managed to rouse the indignation of one of my colleagues. He joked with me in a pleasant way, finding it ridiculous to suggest that young singers hoping to sing Aïda should read Maspero, that those about to sing Dido should read Virgil, and so on. My colleague took my words much too literally. Of course, I do not think it necessary to go prowling through the libraries and to stuff oneself with erudition before singing a scene or a fragment of a role. What I meant to convey—and my witty colleague knew this very well—is that it is necessary to give one's interpretation that indefinable something we commonly call—the expression is far from elegant, but everyone understands it—*local color.* I ask nothing more, but that I insist on.

I simply do not believe that a young interpreter who sings an excerpt from *Aïda,* for example, can communicate—even for a moment—the impression that the scene she is singing takes place in Egypt if she does not hold in her mind's eye, or if she has not held in her mind's eye as she studied the role, some vision of Egypt. If she is solely concerned with her A-flat, her E-natural or the effect that her costume may create, I do not believe that she can transmit to me the image of enormous temples of basalt on the sunlit shores of the Nile.[4]

I do not believe that anyone can sing the role of Henry VIII with the necessary authority, majesty, perfidious courtesy, without first knowing who Henry VIII was and understanding something about his character. Assuming a young singer is vaguely aware that Henry VIII was married six times and had several of his wives killed in order to marry others, that he was a shrewd and formidable politician, I still do not believe this singer will be able to project a satisfactory image of the character if he does not also know that Henry VIII was rotund and blond, that he had pleasing manners and that he concealed his malicious soul under a reassuring stoutness. Why not? Because I know these things, and if this young singer cannot present to my imagination a physical portrait of Henry VIII that corresponds with what I already envision, the impression I receive will be insufficient and incomplete.

Here I am not proposing anything extraordinary; and yet I realize that when one gives this reasonable advice to students, to beginners, there are always others who will tell them: "Pay no attention to such nonsense, concentrate on your *voice!*"

The unhappy result of such advice is before our eyes daily. The unbelievable conceit of the vocal artist, which has always existed but was formerly scorned, is encouraged today; that limit-less conceit is one of the principal causes for the decline of singing today. If singers were not so vain, if they had but the foggiest sense of the evolution of music and art, they would realize that audiences can no longer be content with singing, even faultless singing (which is certainly not the case with their own) that expresses and reflects nothing. We have had our share of squalling baritones or cooing sopranos. The so-called public at large no longer consists exclusively of benevolent bourgeois who nod their heads at little arias or sentimental ladies who swoon because a pomaded tenor has tossed out a robust B-flat. The enormous growth of higher education, the multitude of lectures, the ready availability of books that inform and educate, have created a public at large that is no longer so easy to satisfy. Informed audiences will soon demand that the singers know of what they speak and make a fitting effort to deserve their patronage.

I am somewhat embarrassed to acknowledge the fact, but, in contrast to the ways of the past, it is now in fashionable society above all that one sees that frivolity of judgment and devotion to the faddish which confer stardom on certain singers whose mediocrity would have elicited catcalls from the ordinary people of former times, the "subscribers" who were then the con-noisseurs. But these and related complaints will perhaps provide the topic for another lecture. Today, we must return to the subject of style.

We have seen that the word *style* is misused, that there is no such thing as one style suited to every kind of singing, that indeed there are innumerable styles, and that a good singer must have them all at his or her disposal. We need to replace that inaccurate word *style* with another term, which I will not attempt to locate, but which would signify the whole body of general rules by which singing could be assured of accuracy, gracefulness, correctness and, I might add, a certain "tidiness" which singing can never abandon, even in the most effusive and whimsical moments. This ensemble of rules sums up what I shall temporarily call *vocal style*. It is really a style in itself, suitable for any repertoire. Those who possess it command respect with the very first notes; one immediately recognizes a well-trained singer, master of his art.

To cite only one example among a thousand, I recall the experience of spectators at the Paris Opéra some time ago, during an evening performance of *Lucia di Lammermoor* that marked the debut or the return engagement of Mme Melba. The tenor who was to sing Edgar became ill just before he was to go onstage. What to do? Cancel the performance and refund the money? M. Engel was in the audience and obligingly volunteered to replace the indisposed artist. He took but a few moments to put on his make-up and don a costume that was obviously not made for him and appeared on the stage without ever having rehearsed with his singing partners, thus providing an example of courage and skill beyond the scope of most singers. Everyone was a bit anxious; but the anxiety was short-lived. M. Engel had sung no more than a few notes before everyone was reassured; the calm, the authority, in his diction and his manner of singing, were so impressive that the audience soon felt entirely secure, an uncommon occurrence at the Opéra.

I could not enumerate all the general rules that constitute *vocal style,* so I will limit myself to the principal ones. First, I will comment briefly on correct intonation in singing, then I will discuss *portamentos,* embellishments and rhythm.

Before we consider pitch accuracy, please allow me to draw attention to one of the faults singers should take great care to avoid but to which, unfortunately, most singers are subject. This fault is an excess of sound. It is safe to say that, in general, most people sing too loudly. This past summer, I had a room at the Hôtel des Réservoirs in Versailles. A performance of *Manon* was given at the open-air theater on the far side of the Neptune pond. Well, I assure you that from my room, across a great stretch of the park, I could hear almost everything sung on that stage, the singers shouted so, they howled so at the top of their lungs what should have been sung most discreetly.

Unfortunately, not only this opera, but all operas in the repertoire are performed in this way the world over. Nuances of the voice, revealing the different states of the soul, are totally neglected; familiar conversational tones have all but disappeared from music; singers now strive only for volume of sound. The tenor who sings Des Grieux sings at the same high volume whether he is alone in the anteroom of Saint-Sulpice mourning his lost happiness or at the Hôtel de Transylvanie[5] angrily declaiming his despair.

Typically, one hears passages which should be murmured sung in full voice. And yet, if one looks at the score, one will see *pianissimo* in the orchestral parts and *pianissimo* in the voice line. The composer's intentions are obvious—but do the singers pay any attention? No, they think only of projecting as much sound as they can. Over time, the habit of singing loudly expands the vocal apparatus in all directions; the tissues of the various organs slacken, and it is no longer possible to sing *piano* even if one wished to. Such are the results of a teaching style that is not based on taste, psychology and reason. Once again, it is clear that the mechanics of singing are intimately linked to esthetics.

M. Chaliapin is an admirable example of the expressive power one can achieve by husbanding, conserving, the sound. Never, in a dialogue, does his voice rise above a normal level. He always gives the impression that he holds a supply of voice in reserve, upon which he can draw at the appropriate moment; and this he does at the lyric and dramatic high points, never needing to "force" the sound because, hitherto, he has contained the level of sound with care, and now he needs but a slight boost to create the impression of a powerful contrast.

Now we have come to the matter of accuracy of pitch in singing. Few experiences are as distasteful as hearing someone sing out of tune; but the very best singers, that is, those who have a perfect sense of pitch, may occasionally have a technical accident, a temporary failing that causes them to sing one or two notes out of tune. But to sing out of tune all the time, or even most of the time, is a fatal shortcoming. Such singing is painful for the listeners, but the singer is even more to be pitied because his failing arouses so little compassion.

There are several ways to sing out of tune, or rather, several causes for this calamity, of which I shall cite only the three main ones: first, a bad ear; second, a voice that is out of tune; third, a voice that has been driven out of tune.

If you sing out of tune because you have a bad ear and you cannot hear the sounds you are making, the failing is incurable. The same is true, I believe, if you have a voice that is basically out of tune. In this case, you sing out of tune in a particular way: Not only is each note slightly off, but when you attempt to sing a phrase, you slip from one tonality into another, somewhat like this:

Laisse-moi__ Laisse-moi__ contempler ton vi-sa-ge

I hasten to add that this sort of straying is very rare among professional singers. It occurs only among those whose auditory apparatus has failed or who have suffered a complete loss of voice control, resulting in disorder, chaos, and producing an abominable effect.

If, however, you sing out of tune because your voice has been driven out of tune, the problem can be cured. A voice can be strained and distorted by incorrect technique, by overworking the vocal chords, for example, by singing sharp or flat for long scenes or even continuously. I think that it is easier to correct a voice that tends to go flat than one that goes sharp. But, quite frankly, I am not at all certain that this is true. In any case, there are many inexplicable cases of poor intonation.

Here, by way of example, is a rather curious tale. A few years ago, I was accompanying a very eminent artist in a very familiar selection. Hers had never been a lovely voice, but her singing was extremely interesting. On some occasions, however, no doubt due to fatigue—for she spent a good deal of time teaching—she would sing an entire selection flat. As I accompanied her on this particular day, my task was especially painful, because she sang the whole piece almost half a tone flat. It was painful to accompany her not only because off-pitch singing is offensive to the ear, but also because it conveys a sense of uneasiness and uncertainty. The audience were apparently unaware of her error, or else, for the sake of politeness and out of consideration for the singer's reputation, they did not wish to show it; at any rate, at the end of the selection, they applauded and requested that she repeat it. Taking advantage of the short break and the noise of the ovation, I was careful to play the introduction a semitone lower, thinking that the artist would be more at ease since she had just sung the entire selection a half tone low. Imagine my surprise when I realized that, in spite of my transposition, she again sang a semitone flat!

Obviously, some people sing out of tune with truly extraordinary consistency. Listening to them, one knows at once that they are exceptional musicians, since they are capable of singing entire numbers in a tonality different from the accompaniment, without departing for the blink of an eye from the wrong key they have chosen.

Embellishments in singing are innumerable. We could not hope to note them all; further, their names have changed from one period to another. Also, they have fallen into disfavor today, as they did two or three centuries ago when, first in Italy and then in France, there was a reaction in favor of simple, full-toned singing. Nevertheless, the discreet use of embellishments can add a special pleasure and charm to certain vocal performances. Moreover, since embellishments come in many shapes and forms in the music of every era, it is necessary to recognize and know how to perform them.

Briefly, the most frequently used embellishments are the trill; the turn (which is performed in two ways, starting from the upper or from the lower note); and the mordent. I need not explain the trill here, but will be content to pass on these words of Mme Lilli Lehmann: "Singers who lack agility and the trill, appear to me like horses without tails."

The trill is natural to many singers. Indeed, some singers who lack any other form of agility can produce a trill without effort. On the other hand, singers who after long and serious study succeed in performing the most challenging passages with ease may find it extremely difficult to produce a clear and brilliant trill. The solution, therefore, is to acquire through dogged toil whatever capricious nature first withholds.

The turn is a flexible embellishment performed in the two ways mentioned; it assumes a great diversity of forms. Wagner still used it frequently in expressive vocal and orchestral passages.

The mordent and the inverted mordent (the Italians called this ornament a *mordente,* a particularly complicated form of which was called a *mordente impertinente*) were generally used to confer lightness upon a particular note. The mordent must be executed rapidly and clearly while taking care to give the two notes their true sonority and value despite the rapidity of execution. Like

every other vocal embellishment, the mordent must take its cue
from the nature of the selection being sung and the particular
word it accompanies and must contribute to overall expressiveness. In early music, the mordent frequently appeared in double or
triple form and was subject to numerous variations.

I recall the exquisite shape—slightly mannered, perhaps, but
filled with charm and poetry—that Mme Calvé, her voice more
transparent than crystal, gave to a mordent in the cavatina from *Les
Pêcheurs de Perles* (*The Pearl Fishers*) on the word "*autrefois.*" She
sang this mordent unbelievably slowly and, so to speak, by slightly
separating each note. The effect was delightful, because this
dreamy mordent, accompanying the words "*Comme autrefois*" ("As
in times past") expressed the perfect combination of tenderness
and regret.

Comme au . tre . fois____   Comme au . tre . fois!

There is a much-despised and, in many cases, despicable vocal
practice called *portamento,* "scooping" or "sliding" into a tone. Do
you know what this is? *Portamento* occurs when, in order to go
from one note to another, whether on a single vowel or two
different vowels, whether or not separated by a consonant, the
singer slides the voice from one note to the other, touching on, but
not stopping on, all the intermediate notes, rather than moving the
voice cleanly from one note to another.

Singers cannot totally avoid *portamento,* for without it, their
singing would be too dry. Unconsciously, most singers make
frequent, subtle use of this sliding from note to note, barely
audible sliding which in fact contributes smoothness and connection to singing, which makes *legato* passages possible. But this
subtle sliding should not really be called *portamento.* The real thing
is much more obvious, more conscious. It is a means very often
abused in singing to add expression; but the quality of expression

thus produced very easily becomes whimpering, silly and odiously vulgar.

Yet we should not conclude that *portamento* should be banished entirely. It can produce most gratifying effects, lend charm to singing, add touches that are deliciously unwholesome.

❦

There is one essential quality, whatever music is sung—a quality which almost all singers lack—and that is a sense of rhythm. Nothing is more depressing or irritating than listening to singing without rhythm. This is like walking on uneven ground, covered with bumps and holes, slippery spots and tarpits to fall into—in the end, one judges that it is simply not worth the effort to follow the singer onto this rough terrain where he moves in no clear direction. Alas, there are many who sing in this fashion, who drag one beat then rush the next, slowing down again in the following measure, retarding as if coming to a stop, then suddenly speeding up again, then returning for no reason to a deadly flabbiness and stagnation.

By contrast, nothing gives a greater sense of security, of vigor and ease, than truly rhythmical singing where everything falls in its proper place, singing that picks up at regular intervals, that relates clearly to time and space and moves in a logical progression. There can be no musical delight without rhythm, without cadence, without that pleasant, periodic surge that regulates all the movements of nature, from the turning of the stars to the beating of the heart. Good singing is sustained by steady, firm rhythm, allowing the diction to remain flexible, true, expressive, colorful and confident in its place and time, within the limits set by the rhythm. Thus diction acquires strength and extraordinary power, for the firm boundaries of the rhythm force it to show an ingenuity that makes it all the more interesting.

Rubato is sometimes most valuable and helpful. Do you really know exactly what *rubato* is? Many people think that *rubato,* so often mentioned when one is learning to play a piece by Chopin, consists in rhythmic irregularity, a pressing forward followed by a slowing down, a nervous sort of disorganization. This is a great mistake. Steadiness of rhythm is never more necessary than in a *rubato* passage, for *rubato* consists precisely in the obligation of the artist to balance the rhythm, to slow down immediately after pressing forward, to, by a sort of reflex action, follow each movement with its opposite in order to keep the rhythm securely in place. In a word, *rubato* is the law of rhythmic compensation. After we slow down, we must accelerate to recover the lost time; but through it all, the underlying rhythm must remain invariable, mysteriously inflexible.

Chopin supposedly explained *rubato* thus: "Your left hand plays in time, while your right hand does as it pleases." Singing has neither a right hand nor a left, and yet it has both. Its left hand is the guiding rhythm which is the basis of even the simplest song, while its right hand is the multitude of subtle liberties that may be allowed in a vocal performance.

[1] [Champmeslé (1642–1698), a famous actress and interpreter of the great French dramatist Racine.]

[2] [Mme Viardot-Garcia (1821–1910), mezzo-soprano, appeared in Berlioz's arrangement of Gluck's *Orfeo* in Paris in 1859.]

[3] To select a famous or eminent artist as a model is all very well. Unfortunately, our examples are becoming rarer and rarer. Seven years have passed since I wrote these lines, but I have yet to hear a Salammbô young sopranos might do well to imitate.

[4] One may object that the composer of *Aïda* did not himself pay much attention to local color, being more preoccupied by emotion than by the picturesque. All

the same, the drama takes place in Egypt, and opera is replete with instances where it falls to the interpreters to fill the gaps left by the composers.

[5] [A fashionable gambling house in Paris and the setting of Act IV of Massenet's *Manon.*]

Fedor Chaliapin, Russian bass (1873–1938), in the title role of Boito's *Mefistofele*. Reproduced from the Collections of the Library of Congress.

V

How to Move an Audience

Mesdames, Mesdemoiselles, Messieurs,

During our first meeting, we explored the impulses that inspire human beings to sing. If we did not succeed in identifying them all, at least we discovered enough to spend an entire hour together. At the second meeting, we attempted to treat the basic mechanisms of vocal performance. In the third session, we dealt with certain aspects of diction. I believe I was able to give sound advice based on well-known, proven and, so to speak, unassailable principles. My task was a bit harder in the last lecture, because I was attempting not only to define *style*, but also to discuss a few widespread opinions relating to the amount of respect we owe to singing traditions.

Today, I am faced with a question that is more bothersome yet: How is a singer to move an audience? The range of the human sensibility is staggering; the degrees and kinds of emotions vary with each individual, and this inherent multiplicity of feelings is continuously affected by evolving times and customs, by the infinite diversity among continents, countries, villages and neighborhoods. You can readily understand that I must find some way to limit this subject, lest we find ourselves still in this lecture hall after the modern sensibility has taken yet another major turn!

Therefore, with your permission, we are going to turn towards the past, to examine a variety of bygone eras, with the aim of finding and agreeing on a handful of emotions that have persisted through the centuries in the human heart and that can still be animated today as they were in the past. We shall also investigate different means of stirring these persistent emotions.

To begin with, we should note that some people are extremely sensitive, while others are not so in the least. One day Liszt gave a masterful recital, playing without interruption for almost an hour some of the most beautiful selections from Beethoven, Mozart and Schumann; the audience was deeply moved. All the same, one man in the group could find nothing better to say than: "Does it not hurt your fingers to hit the keys like that?".

In contrast, I know a young woman who is not only especially responsive to music, but who expresses her own emotions in the most bizarre ways. One day, wishing to compliment me on my song "L'Heure exquise," which I had just performed in the most ethereal possible way, she exclaimed: "Ah, such music! It's like a kick in the stomach!" Indeed, many people wrongly believe that art, to deliver its full quotient of emotion, should also deliver a kick in the gut.

Composers, too, often make this mistake, which explains the existence of so many frantic compositions in which passion, violence, uproar and maladjustment compete furiously for the honor of alarming, dismaying, deafening and intoxicating the listener. Those who rely on such intensity fail to appreciate the value of subtly shaded feelings, the often immense satisfaction of a light and fleeting emotion, the delicious sorrow of quiet tears, the sweetness of a sigh and the exquisite, bitter charm of melancholy. They cannot see the despair in a smile, or the sadness in a ray of sunlight. Let us leave them to their own raptures, while we remain unashamed to take pleasure in modest emotions, feelings common to all men, and to venerate the sublime coterie of artists whose works bespeak serenity and balance. These artists alone know that it is a sin against art to deliver repeated kicks to the stomach; and they hold in contempt the kinds of emotions these pugilistic methods inspire.

∽✒︎∾

Literally, in medical terms, the word *emotion* signifies a disturbance in one's psychological state. Inducing such a disturbance, ever so mildly, even covertly, creates an "emotion." Quite frequently, singers with the most remarkable voices and with the greatest appeal due to their vocal talent and skill are at the same time thoroughly boring. Their work is technically excellent but dull and vaguely soporific. These singers not only do not feel what they are singing, they do not think as they sing, and that is why they fail to move the listener; their singing is inept and inexpressive.

A singer must hold before his eyes, as he sings, an image, whether sharp or dim, of what the words he is pronouncing suggest. If the words allude to objects, the singer must see them while singing; only then will he be able to transmit this vision to the listener. If the words describe a state of mind, the singer must delve into his own experience, must search inwardly for all that is deeply felt and human, and must create in his own mind the very attitude he wishes to convey—he must experience, at that moment, the emotion he seeks to express.

This is not the time to expound upon Diderot's *Paradoxe sur le Comédien* or the endlessly repeated discussions to which this work has given rise; we will not ask ourselves whether the actor or singer (for even the singer performing without a costume, holding his music in his hand, is an actor) must or must not feel what he expresses—this question would carry us too far. But I must point out that if, while singing, the singer had to feel the full power of the emotions he interprets—if he were truly overcome with hilarity or tortured by pain—he would not be able to sing.

We are told that on occasion, Mme Malibran, as she left the stage, had fits of hysteria because she was overstimulated by her own singing; I believe this. But when we are told that as she sang, she shed genuine tears, I do not believe it. Even those great artists who are the most impetuous and easily carried away have a point in the brain which remains lucid and under voluntary control. (On this subject, you will find some most interesting comments in an article by Sainte-Beuve about Racine, in the *Nouveaux Lundis,* I believe). You may be sure that if Mme Malibran shed tears onstage, they dried up the moment she had to sing a vocalise (and in the music of her repertoire, these were plentiful). Of course, the same is not the case for actors in *spoken* drama: They can, with impunity, abandon themselves to their tears; their sobbing may delay their delivery or make it jerky, but it only enhances its poignancy.

At present, Mme Sarah Bernhardt offers an admirable example of such sublime abandon. In *Jeanne Doré,* when she arrives at the tribunal to plead for her son, she cries so long and with such wrenching tears that she can hardly speak and must sometimes stop between words, her voice carried away by the emotions flowing from her heart. That marvelous and shattering spectacle is repeated every evening. By what mysterious means can Mme Sarah Bernhardt appear nightly in this state of abject discomposure, while remaining in perfect command of her mental powers? She may well agree to share her secret with you, in this hall, when she comes to address you. As for me, I shall not even attempt to discover it: It is a sacrilege to seek to unveil the mysteries of genius for the sole purpose of satisfying one's prideful curiosity.

But, I repeat, when it comes to singing, such excesses would be disastrous. Deepest emotion may invade the singer to the point of making his voice tremble, but it must not make it impossible for him to sing.

You know, of course, that nothing (and here I speak rather crudely), nothing stimulates the mucous membranes of the nose quite like crying; sobbing cuts off the flow of breath; the jerks and spasms of acutely felt pain interfere with the smooth support of the sound. And these observations are confirmed by the famous example of Mme Desbordes-Valmore, who wrote that she had to give up her singing career because her singing made her cry. It may be that a singer does not cry, yet he sometimes makes others cry, while retaining, to a point, his self-control. On the other hand, those who believe that one can stimulate emotion in others without experiencing the slightest feeling oneself—that one can remain cold, totally aloof, and yet ignite a spark, totally dry-eyed and yet summon tears—those people are sadly deceived, as they ascribe to the artist a power belonging only to the rod of Moses.

These remarks bring to mind an anecdote that may amuse you and that I guarantee to be true, although I am neither willing nor able to name the heroes. A famous French actor was talking one day with a famous American actor and told him that, onstage, he remained completely cold, detached from the sentiments of the characters he portrayed, and that he appealed to the sensibilities of the audience solely by virtue of his talent and his technical mastery. In support of his assertion, he added: "In the play *L'Aventurière,* at the moment when I supposedly fall asleep at the table, it frequently happens that I really doze off, until Fabrice taps me on the shoulder. This awakens me, and I begin acting again."

"Yes," his interlocutor replied coolly, "and then it is our turn to fall asleep."

I believe, in fact I am sure (and recently, my friend M. Henry Bernstein, a man of authority, supported this view in conversation), that in order to convey emotion, one must enter into an altered state which is neither a complete and absolute abandonment of self, nor one's native personality, nor a cold and clever self-control. One must split off a different personality, but one must do it quite consciously. It is this ability to combine two distinct mental states that defines the talent of a singer.

That talent may be used and displayed in several ways. Some singers—Mme Krauss, for example, or Mme Malibran—are most secure in their technique and thorough in their preparation; yet when they perform, they will suddenly begin to improvise and, thanks to genuine inspiration, produce some surprising effects. These sudden changes, these abrupt shifts of approach, often hinge on the tiniest details of circumstance. Other singers, on the other hand, those whose mind dominates their psyche (Fauré, for example), after thoroughly thinking through the psychological combinations that will permit them to convey the desired emotion, will pursue this course undeviatingly, without the slightest change.

Certain singers hoard and dispense their emotion with uncanny skill and prudence, so that a slight change of voice, a tiny increase in the intensity of the diction, is enough to evoke strong feeling. M. Chaliapin can be numbered among these singers. All the information I can gather about Mme Carvalho indicates that she too belonged to this privileged group of artists, but she worked in a totally different way, since she was concerned chiefly with the delicate and discreet emotions. What would I not have given to hear her sing the first act of *Faust:* "Non, Monsieur," and so on. I am told that a shiver of pleasure passed through the hall.

There is still a third category of singers: those who possess *charm* and who, without even trying, without a moment's thought (and this is a function of the quality of their singing as much as a function of the atmosphere they create), impart to the music, even when pronouncing unimportant words, tender and warm emotion.

A singer who personifies this particular type is M. Jean de Reszke: Even in heroic moments, when he projected virile, powerful emotions, his singing retained an affectionate, convincing inflection which, never cloying or insipid, only made his singing more enticing. I remember that in *Le Prophète,* when he exclaimed: "King of the Heavens and of the Angels!" there was in his voice not only the exaltation of the warrior about to rush into battle, but also the tender humility of the young Saint John, bringing his weakness to the bosom of the Savior.

Let us turn now to certain *belles époques* of music to see what kinds of emotions were considered most rare and exquisite, most worthy of artistic pursuit. This will necessitate a small journey into history and will help to console me for having spoken so little, in the course of these lectures, about the evolution of vocal art. We will not go back too far—only to the beginning of the 17th century, when, in Italy, there was a reaction against polyphony, the form of vocal art in favor up to that time, which was led by such great artists as Peri, Caccini and Monteverdi and which gave birth to opera.

I will not encumber this lecture with the tale of opera's step-by-step development (for this you can turn to such fine studies as that by M. Romain Rolland). Singing, under the influence of those exceptional leaders whom we shall call the early masters of dramatic music, assumed a sober but expressive character, in which vocalization (that is to say, vocal lightness, flexibility) played a relatively insignificant role. This new genre, which required very special training, prevailed for many years, leading to all sorts of strife and controversy, after which there was a gradual revival of vocal virtuosity. Eager to again hold sway, virtuosity superimposed itself little by little upon the simple, pure art of the early Italian masters and added to the broad, declamatory recitations (which generally introduced the selections) "bravura" arias in which the voice could sparkle and excel, performing extremely difficult passages which could quickly establish the reputation of a singer.

Increasingly, the main purpose of these arias was to display the singer's virtuosity. Thus virtuosity became more and more central to dramatic music and, in the second half of the 18th century, succeeded in dominating it almost completely. Beautiful, serene melodic lines disappeared, and extravagant embellishments reigned supreme. At this point, singers who remembered the art of the early period began to deplore the disappearance of *bel canto*. The teachers of the art of singing in these later years have come down to us as grumblers, muttering against prevailing tastes and bemoaning the loss of the beautiful vocal tradition that constituted the foundation of expressive singing, both tuneful and declamatory, for the better part of the 17th century and the beginning of the 18th.

Many people today confuse *bel canto* with Romantic music, which developed later, in the first five decades of the 19th century. Let us try to bring some order to this confusion. I believe that *bel canto,* properly speaking, was less concerned with the spiritual interpretation of works than with perfecting the lightness and flexibility of the voice, the delivery of the melodic phrase. Its aim was an infinitely varied tone quality, an impeccable purity of pronunciation; in short, it sought to obtain from the vocal apparatus, independently of any emotional factors, everything possible in terms of sonority and the purely physical realization of sound. Everyone agreed that the pleasure of hearing a beautiful, well-disciplined voice was sufficient in itself; or, rather, that a beautiful, well-disciplined voice was what was needed above all to best serve the music and to move the listener. Of course, singers who were artists of real stature and refinement were not content with a merely physical realization; they lifted their performance to a higher level of beauty through the exercise of intelligence, taste and feeling. But, once again, their primary objective was perfection in beautiful singing—in *bel canto*.

This *bel canto* was not chiefly concerned with rapid vocal execution or acrobatic perfection; it was later that these qualities came to be appreciated above others. And therein, precisely, lies the difference between *bel canto* and the Romantic school.

What was particularly sought after in *bel canto* was a certain tonal quality: a smoothness and flexibility of sound, the ability of the singer to produce not just three, four or five sonorities, but as many as ten, twenty, thirty. The singer had to be able to sculpt his voice, to subject it to an endless stream of tonal variations without disturbing its steady flow, to shade it with every color of the musical prism.

To this end, voice teachers used a variety of different methods. Each had his own system and his fanciful notions, as is perhaps best exemplified in the story of Porpora and his student Caffarelli, who was later to become the greatest and best-known singer of his time. Fascinated by the young Caffarelli's talents, Porpora, who was the undisputed grand master of singing in Italy (you may know this, Mesdemoiselles, if you have read *Consuelo*), was also, for a time, Haydn's instructor—without doubt, a most eminent teacher. Porpora wrote down a few simple exercises, seemingly so easy that present-day students at the Conservatoire would disdain them, thinking them far beneath them. He directed Caffarelli to work on this page of exercises very slowly, not for weeks, not for a few months, but for *four years* without ever permitting him to sing something else, exploding with rage and threatening to cane him when the young man showed signs of impatience. When, finally, the student sang that page of exercises slowly, perfectly and in such a way that Porpora could find nothing to correct—that is to say, when sound and performance were impeccable—Porpora said to Caffarelli: "Go, I can teach you nothing else. You are the greatest singer of our day."

With these words, he did not mean that Caffarelli had attained the supreme level of artistic achievement; he did not intend to say: "Now you can perform, you can tackle stage works, you can outshine all your colleagues." What he meant was: "Now you are ready to begin the study of vocal art in its entirety; now you are in possession of an incomparable vocal foundation, a set of perfect principles that will permit you to sing everything and, little by little, to rise to the highest level of your art."

Many who have heard this anecdote have failed to understand its meaning: They have concluded that Porpora considered this single page of exercises sufficient to train an artist. We know these exercises were very simple and slow, were not even, in truth, vocalises. When Porpora asked his pupil to sing them many times each day, very slowly, it was undoubtedly to watch very closely every aspect of his breathing: how the sound originated, how it developed, how it expanded; all this in order to give him complete control over the shaping of a sound, in order to "break in" that voice like a new pair of shoes, to bring it totally under the control of the singer, to make it responsive to his slightest whim. Porpora was convinced that given such training, the voice would be ready to cope with ever-greater technical difficulties and capable of conveying every shade of expression.

For *bel canto* was also concerned with expression. You know what it means to *stylize*. This term has been used excessively in recent years, and misused almost as frequently. *Stylization* is that artistic process by which one modifies or distorts, for decorative reasons, the things one represents. For example, to stylize a flower, a plant, an insect, a bird, one would, without stripping the model of its essential characteristics, change its contours in such a way as to lend it a harmony and balance appropriate to decorative purposes.

Bel canto operated in a similar way. I do not believe that it allowed realism of vocal expression; but I do believe that the singers drew inspiration from the text, from the external verbal forms, drew out the essential part and embellished and ennobled it through singing. Expression had its place in *bel canto,* but it was not excessive, not exaggerated; it lacked the stark realism that Gluck would later require of his interpreters. The feeling was sorrowful—but moderate; or it was joyful—but moderate. It would have been an affront to the beauty of singing, to the nobility of the vocal rite, to embrace too lowly and human an element. Thus, all that beautiful singing, those beautiful sounds, the entire harmonious and melodious construction, were pervaded by feeling, every feeling, and every thought, but were always subjected to this transformation, this vocal stylization.

And that, Mesdemoiselles, is what *bel canto* was. Lully, disciple of the early Italian masters of opera, introduced their melodic and declamatory style into France while forcing it to conform to that solemn regularity so cherished in his time. But I spoke about Lully the last time we met, so I will not return to that subject.

Rameau, and later Gluck, approached expression quite differently. In Rameau's dramatic scenes, despite their considerable dignity, the singer can permit himself more realism. Rameau belonged to the age of the *Encyclopédie;* he was interested in the totality of human nature, its contrasting beauty and ugliness, its violences and weaknesses. He did not always succeed in bringing his characters to vibrant life; his long dialogues were still highly stylized, and the conventions of declamation—proper, moderate and measured—still largely respected. But sometimes, suddenly, a gust of realism rushes in to disturb the majestic folds of finery, to scatter the theatrical paraphernalia, blow away the masks and the wigs. At that moment, living humanity emerges, as in the scene from *Castor et Pollux* when Pollux, in an admirable gesture, implores Jupiter to let him go down to Hades to bring back his brother Castor. It would be absurd to sing this passage with the studied decorum of *bel canto.*

* * * * * * * * * *

Gluck presents a different challenge for the singer. While he imparts a much greater realism to his music, Gluck, at the same time, inserts in his effusions, his frenzies, his brusque transports, a melodious lyricism, a melodic continuity (you notice how I insist on the word *melody*), a manner of singing that may be ill-suited to the impassioned moods of realism. Gluck's recitatives, which, most of the time, closely observe the prosody of the spoken language, are infinitely easier to sing than his cantilenas. I admit that I find these Gluck cantilenas most admirable. The noble and ingratiating aspects of the melodic line compete, in the pursuit of emotion, with all the expressive resources of spoken discourse; but it is not simple to bring out the beauty of these cantilenas while endowing them with a large portion of emotion and truth. If there is too much speech-like emphasis, the plasticity of the melodic line is destroyed; if there is too much singing emphasis, expression is weakened. When I say that those arias are difficult, it is because I have heard them sung so badly; on the other hand, when I say that Gluck's recitatives are less difficult to interpret, it is probably because I have forgotten the pitiful way in which they are usually performed.

The concern for genuine, moving expression is rare among today's singers. I have quoted Mme Lilli Lehmann's words to the effect that she did not consider herself ready to sing a certain aria by Beethoven because, after working at it for seventeen years, she still had not mastered it. Today, such an attitude is rare indeed.

If, occasionally, in my writings about the Conservatoire, I seem to be unduly nasty, it is because I know very well that most of the students (some of whom are quite gifted and could become remarkable artists) are vain and completely indifferent to the art with which they should be proud to be involved. Such an "artist" comes to my mind: a woman who is admired because she is pretty and has a brilliant voice. But she condescends to come to rehearsals, arrives late, does not know her role and pays little heed to the two or three timid observations offered by the conductor. She rehearses nonchalantly and dashes out with a rustling of silk and clinking of trinkets, for she must go to two fittings and several other appointments before dinner. On the evening of the performance, she thinks only of her costume. Her singing, the character she interprets, the artistic effects she might strive for, the emotion she might seek to convey, all are irrelevant to her. She is sure she will find flattering reviews in the newspapers the next day, and, once the performance is done, she does not think about her role or her singing until the next one. Who is to say she is wrong? The public supports her, and after two or three years of this dazzling and unproductive life, she will be off to America in spite of the laments of her ignorant admirers.

Believe me, a singer cannot develop a talent in this way, but only through never-ending attention to his or her profession, to his or her *métier*. When we really love singing, everything we see, everything we hear, serves our art. We relate every aspect of our daily life to our precious vocation, which is with us at each moment. A phrase comes to mind: We sing it again and again to ourselves, trying to draw from it all the musical and poetic effects possible. We repeat it a thousand times; we change the shape of a vowel, the intensity of a consonant; we start anew; we search for a more authentic accent: "No! That's not it . . . This is better . . . This is an affectation . . . This is too dry . . . I could perhaps do it this way . . . but, is it *human,* is it real?" And so we reflect on and on. We identify with the character we are to portray; we ardently experience the emotions we wish to convey, we look at them from every side, we examine our soul and compare it with that of others. If we could, we would penetrate to the very core of the human heart to find the secrets of expression. At the same time, we look for the sound that translates the thought, the sound that is its measure, the sound that makes it manifest in all its crystal beauty. In a word, *we concentrate on singing.* Thoughts of singing never leave us, and we live, night and day, with this companion who forever tries to escape us, but to whom we cling with all the strength of despair and all the persistence of desire.

In Gluck's works, expression is always put to the use of grandiose, epic or fabulous subjects; his characters are Orpheus, Iphigenia, Agamemnon, Renaud, Clytemnestra, Alcestis. These are major figures whose mythic stature forbids any thought of familiarity. Their feelings and their deeds (and you know that Gluck, in his music, makes abundant use of deeds to transmit feelings, that he persistently resorts to external effects, in the manner of the true stage director)—their feelings and their deeds have a grandeur and power far beyond the reach of ordinary humanity.

Such is not the case in Mozart's works. He was an artist such as may appear two or three times in a century, an artist with a God-given sense of proportion who instinctively turned away from excess in any form and who was able to combine the most opposite qualities in perfect equilibrium, to unite them in a new and perfectly harmonious whole. Moreover, the subjects that he chose and the characters to whom he gave voice compelled him to remain within the bounds of ordinary life, even in exuberantly lyrical moments.

Therefore, when performing Mozart's works, one must make every effort to remain true in the strict sense of the word: true to familiar, everyday life, and not to some grander concept, to the magnified scale of fable or epic.

One can proceed in this fashion with no fear of making Mozart sound dull or ordinary. You may be sure that Mozart's music itself provides the necessary portion of beauty, embellishes to exactly the right degree and no more those ordinary feelings and the accents that translate them. To convey the proper emotion in singing Mozart, it is necessary only to respect the full and exact value of the musical phrase and the rhythm as this master conceived them, to in no way set up obstructions.

* * * * * * * * * *

Lilli Lehmann, German soprano (1848–1929), as Brünnhilde in Wagner's *Ring*. Courtesy Photo Archive of Benedikt & Salmon Record Rarities, San Diego.

VI

Some Causes of the Decline of Singing

Mesdames, Mesdemoiselles, Messieurs,

Your eagerness to attend yet another series of my lectures on singing is a mark of appreciation that makes me proud and moves me deeply.

We will resume what I shall describe, with a pun from Berlioz, as a promenade *"à travers chant,"*[1] sauntering somewhat at random across the vast and rich domain of vocal art which we explored and of which we defined the general topography a few months back. We shall pause at the most pleasant spots to enjoy their charms, but we shall also stop in certain arid regions to survey and define the terrain, the soil, whatever is surprising and particular. During these wanderings, we will visit many points that I have already mentioned or described; but since there is no further need to explain their nature, we shall have ample time to focus on details, to take a complete tour. This manner of proceeding, by starts and stops, is a detriment to keeping things in order; but it has, at least, the advantage of variety, and I do pray that you will not refuse to pay close attention simply because I do not proceed in a formal way.

Today, I will look into the principal causes of that much-discussed decline of the art of singing which all have agreed to deplore.

❦

Many, indeed, have pondered its cause. A thousand different explanations have been offered for the scarcity of singers and their mediocrity. Not all of these are plausible, but there is some truth to most of them. Some people blame bad teaching, and they are probably not entirely wrong; others blame the modern repertoire. There can be no doubt that need will create the instrument; and so, if today's music required a genuine vocal science, that science would be reborn and would soon flourish again as it did when the "modern" music of times past could not do without genuine *singers*.

Still other commentators vigorously assert that the Wagnerian school has been disastrous for singing, but they are wrong. Since we have touched ever so lightly on the pitfalls that modern music holds out for the voice, please allow me to point out the fact that the good, the true, the great Wagnerian singers have maintained their voices, their ability, their artistic activity into a fairly advanced age. I have heard Vogl, near sixty, in the role of Tristan at Bayreuth, and though his voice was somewhat uneven (as it has always been), it still possessed an irresistible ardor and charm. I have heard the great Materna singing Brünhilde and Isolde, the most challenging roles of the Wagnerian repertoire, when she was well past her youth. Mme Lilli Lehmann, whose sixtieth birthday was joyously celebrated by a group of fellow artists just a few years ago, sang Wagner roles all her life and still sings them incomparably, as she does everything else in her repertory.

We should be aware that, when the great lyric revolution of the mid-19th century took place, the singers caught up in it were experienced artists molded in the *Italian school*. They did not await the arrival of Wagner or his compositions to begin their singing careers; they had cut their teeth on Handel, Bach, Mozart, Cimarosa, Gluck, Beethoven, and the Italian Romantics: Bellini, Rossini and their followers. Their healthy voices, their skill and technique, enabled them to sing the so-called "music of the future" without damaging their voices. More than that, thanks to the technique of *legato* singing, which they had practiced since their youth, they could draw from that music all the melodic and lyric wealth it contains, which is immense.

What led audiences at one time to believe that this music lacked melody was the fact that melody was introduced and developed in a manner unknown up to that time. In the earlier, so-called melodic operas, the accompaniment (to use a word that is easily understood) was neutral; it existed solely to support the singing and keep it on pitch and in time. In itself, it had no meaning, no physiognomy or shape; it had no expressive role to play. One must go back to Mozart (one must always return to him, because all that is musical is found in Mozart) to discover, not the equivalent, but the premonition, the source, of the polyphonic style familiar to us all today.

Even Beethoven, the brilliant symphonist who could make instruments speak so as to wring tears from the heart—even in the works of Beethoven, who so intently used every means to add to the expressiveness of the words, the accompaniment is rarely expressive in itself and on its own account, though it often serves to emphasize the vocal line.

With Mozart, the accompaniment is rarely so detached; only in the rare case does it remain apart from the feeling expressed by the voice or the words. As an example, let us take the entrance of Donna Elvira in the first act of *Don Giovanni*. But here, I choose to tarry for a moment.

The role of Elvira has the reputation of being a poor one, a sacrificial role. Actually, it is an admirable role. Gustave Moreau[2] once paid me the honor of inviting me to his home, where he spoke at length about *Don Giovanni*. He believed that Don Ottavio and Elvira were the two best-delineated characters in Mozart's drama. In his opinion, it is easier to give musical expression to sentiments that go far beyond the normal range of human emotion than to ordinary feelings familiar to every human soul. It requires a keen musical sense to confer upon these humble feelings, lacking excess of any sort, nobility and beauty.

This is exactly what Mozart does for the role of Elvira. As soon as this amorous, jealous woman appears onstage, the orchestral *ritornello* (introduction) paints a precise picture of her character. Of course, the moment she starts to sing, her voice adds a touching, tender quality; but the accompaniment, as we have agreed to call it, suffices in itself to give us a clear idea of Elvira. One sees that she is beautiful and gentle, calm, essentially normal, but completely overcome by love. The violins and violas embody the sharp claws of her jealousy, the palpable emotions that she would unleash upon Don Giovanni if he were in her presence. It is obvious that Elvira would not be content with sad and dignified reproaches, that she would not hesitate to make a real scene. She speaks of "piercing the heart of this impious one," of setting "a shocking example"; this she declares with cries of rage and brusque silences, as she savors her plans for vengeance. But in spite of these ignoble outbursts, the musical language does not for a moment lose its character of ideal purity.

Meanwhile, Don Giovanni, who has failed to recognize his own "wife" under her mantilla, already burns with passion for this alluring, unknown woman. "It must be some belle, forsaken by her lover," he whispers to Leporello, as the orchestra characterizes the qualities of the great lover—caressing, insinuating, imitating his glances and his sinuous gestures. Don Giovanni decides at once to console the lovely stranger. The short motif accompanying the words, "Let us calm her torments," has a delightful charm, a perfectly modern form and expression. I see here one of those sudden, prophetic flashes of inspiration which loom up in the art of the 18th century, one of those memorable moments that rise above the exquisitely rational tradition of the time to plant a seed of poetry for the future.

As the voice and the singing assume more importance in the music of the theater, the accompaniment declines in importance until, among bad composers, it is reduced to mere rhythmic fluttering, to lifeless patterns with neither force nor character. Even in the music of the masters, expression and musical impetus are concentrated in the vocal line. In Weber's works, for example, in spite of the fact that he gave the orchestra extraordinary energy and authority, one frequently finds accompaniments like the following[3] to support the speaking and singing voice:

Méhul, who can be so moving and so human, provides his most expressive cantilenas with accompaniments that are incredibly remote and bland. Consider this example:[4]

Or this one:[5]

I need not dwell on the Italians, whose muse is purely vocal and melodic. For them, the accompaniment is of no importance whatsoever. I will not go so far as to say that it could have been omitted entirely, but it could have been altered in radical and contradictory ways without doing harm to the music. Take this example:[6]

Or:[7]

The operatic public was familiar with such passive forms of accompaniment. They knew that the melody was in the voice part; that is where they sought it and where they found it. So the public was utterly disconcerted when the melody began to come from everywhere at the same time, spreading and extending in all directions, yet forming a harmonious, indivisible whole. The listener's ear, importuned from all sides, was at first bewildered, panic-stricken by this resounding sphere of interwoven melodies; it no longer knew which way to turn to isolate a single tune. For many years, the public therefore believed that melody was missing from this music, while in fact it was there in great abundance.

I repeat, I do not believe that the Wagnerian school had anything to do with the decline of singing. Let us look elsewhere. First of all, if we wish to focus on purely artistic causes, we must not overlook a very important factor (and I am not the first to point it out): the disappearance of church choirs (*maîtrises*). The baneful consequences of this historic decline have been pointed out for some years.

As you are well aware, for centuries, the parish choirs were the true nurseries for singers. Young boys with pleasant voices were given not only *solfeggio* instruction, but also genuine vocal training; their voices were developed in parallel with their tastes, and when they reached that painful time in adolescence when they shed their boyhood voices, they had already learned a great deal. Once their voices had changed, those who still possessed a facility for singing were eager to resume their studies and were equally eagerly accepted into church and monastery schools. As choirboys, they had acquired the fundamentals of vocal technique as well as musical taste; now they could reap the benefits of their hard work. Music, singing, were not a strange world filled with obstacles. From the cradle, they had been surrounded by music, nourished in the rites and the love of singing; and nothing is more enduring or important than the first, formative experiences of childhood.

Unfortunately, I had no personal experience with religious choir schools, but my scanty experience with their style of discipline was enough to convince me of the educational value of an apprenticeship in the repertoire of sacred vocal music. As a child, I had a soprano voice with a rather extended range; I could easily reach D above high C. My teacher and very dear friend, Lucien Grandjany, a young man with a genuine talent for teaching who died at the age of twenty-nine, was organist at the church of Saint-Vincent-de-Paul, where he occasionally allowed me to sing. My eagerness to display my voice and the deep satisfaction that congratulatory comments gave to my youthful ego were incentive enough to encourage me to ever-better performances, to a casual search for new and better means to achieve resonance or expression. Without realizing it, I became familiar with the art of singing as I sang these beautiful sacred songs, accompanied by the calm and true strains of the organ (for, with the organ, one cannot cheat, one cannot conceal the weaknesses of a singer by heavy use of pedaling, as is possible with the piano).

Singing the sacred repertoire is a wonderful exercise. In church, one must sing in a sustained, *legato* way, avoiding any brusqueness or irregularity. Religious song must conform to the solemn environment in which it is performed, whether its purpose is to humbly implore divine mercy, to bring consolation and hope to the soul or to clearly and purely glorify God's majesty. Usually, this kind of singing must preserve a perfect serenity, even in moments of brilliance. So, when subjected to that kind of apprenticeship, it would be the rare singer who did not develop an instinct for sustained and *legato* singing, which is to say, for *singing* itself. When one has learned that style, when one has mastered it, one is capable, technically speaking, of singing almost anything. It is a foundation, a base, that has no equal.

Furthermore, when singing in church, one develops what I might call the capacity for vocal self-effacement, or, if you prefer, humility in the presence of music. As the music requires, one does not hesitate to give precedence to another vocal line or to function as an anonymous part of the choral fabric, to serve modestly, yet with accuracy and fervor, the musical work as a whole, to observe the delicacies of nuance and proportion, all of which, later, greatly aid vocal interpretation.

Today's singers, however, have not ventured onto these proving grounds. The theater is their principal goal, and most begin their study at an age when the preoccupations of daily life are already paramount, when they are already driven by ambition. Caught up in the fast pace that marks the present world, these young singers, some of them very talented, study quickly, inattentively, motivated only by a shallow desire to advance themselves. That childhood initiation, that naïve burgeoning of faith in the art they must master, are lacking. As long as they are building a "reputation," arriving at some forced, premature success, they are perfectly satisfied. At the Conservatoire, only one thing matters: to score a brilliant success in the competition at the end of the academic year. In singing a selection or scene, the students make no effort to fathom the musical meaning, the sentiment or message of their chosen selection.[8] Their only concern is to duplicate the vocal formula of last year's winning singer.

And so, our presumptuous youngsters make their debut. But here we encounter another serious cause, perhaps the most serious, of the decline of singing. Please believe me, I say this without bitterness, without the slightest desire to offend, but with a simple and far-reaching sadness: This major cause of decline is the incompetence of the public.

There was a time when the audiences filling the theaters knew, when they heard a singer, how to assess his or her real merit. Why? Because, in general, everyone loved singing and was interested in it to some degree; from childhood onward, it was customary to really listen to singers. The musical theater was, at that time, a favorite entertainment. That is where one sought distraction from work, where one spent an evening as soon as time and means permitted. The singers, aware they they were being competently listened to, observed and assessed, proceeded with care from the very beginning, made every possible effort to earn the approval of the public and, in particular—I insist upon this point—the approbation of the young. Thus they paved the way for glorious and fruitful careers. How many times have I heard older people today, remembering their youth, say: "As soon as I had a little money in my pocket, I would buy a ticket for the Opéra, the Théâtre des Italiens or the Théâtre Lyrique in order to hear Mario,[9] Frezzolini,[10] Fauré or Mme Carvalho!"

After performances in which so many excellent singers participated, young operagoers would analyze, discuss and debate the merits or weaknesses of this or that performer. This mood of excitement, this effervescence, this informed gaiety, created an atmosphere in which the art of singing flourished.

Let me tell you a little story.

A few wealthy and busy gentlemen gathered in a restaurant owned by a well-known gourmet and ordered a very old and fine brandy from a region of France near Cognac. As they spoke of business matters, they began to drink it hurriedly. Noticing this lack of savoir-faire, the owner said: "Gentlemen, what are you doing? One does not drink good brandy in such a way!"

"How does one drink it?" they asked.

"First, one warms the glass in one's hand, swirls the liqueur in the glass, then one savors the aroma, then finally one takes a taste, and then . . ."

"And then?"

"And then, gentlemen, one *talks about it.*"

The same applies to music and singing. As a painting must be appreciated in the light, music must be appreciated in silence and leisure. First, one must really listen. Singing is a mystery that vanishes the moment it is created. To grasp its magic, to capture its greatest beauties, one must pay it scrupulous and passionate attention. After it has been truly heard, after its beauties have been tenderly collected and stored in memory, it must be summoned forth again, recaptured from the ether where it vanished at its birth; all the impressions it evoked must be revived. In a phrase, one must *think about it.*

In the intimate process of gathering the music into oneself, a kind of communion is established in the concert hall between listener and singer, and this in turn encourages the singer's efforts. But this communion and the atmosphere it creates are absent from theaters today. Why? Because the present generation of young people, so intelligent, so bold, rich in expectations and capable of soaring enthusiasms, invests its interest in matters far removed from music and especially singing. Young people no longer possess a real love for singing; they pay no attention to it and thus have no knowledge of it. This lack of knowledge leads to an indifferently developed ear, which is easily satisfied or repelled. The art of singing grows feeble and slowly dies.

And what explains this absence of love for singing among today's young people? This is simply because they love many other things, because our present era is devoted to mechanical gadgets and sports. Is this bad? Certainly not, since many of our brightest minds are delighted to see our young people practice this religion of the muscle with such fervor and since the manufacturing industries are a major source of national prosperity. But that which constitutes the wealth and power of a nation is rarely conducive to its artistic greatness, and those who cherish singing cannot help deploring the preoccupations and activities of today's youth which are so inimical to the cultivation of this delightful art.

And so the young singer makes his or her debut. Often, the promising qualities of the voice, which is still evolving and full of faults, go unnoticed, while a knowledgeable audience would recognize them and encourage their development. The reaction in the hall is cold, hostile. The beginner, disappointed and neglected, has neither the desire nor the opportunity to progress in his art. He will remain a mediocre singer simply because he was neither supported nor enlightened with sound advice.

But, in fact, what happens still more often is this: Thanks to a few showy natural gifts, a perfectly ignorant singer makes a favorable impression when he or she first appears before an ignorant public. A handsome appearance, a few striking notes and some two dozen friends in the hall are all one needs to launch a career today. Soon, the name of the beginner appears in musical publications with such epithets as "an admirable Carmen," "a marvelous Manon," "a delightful Roméo." Many times I have naïvely let myself be tempted by such accolades, which I wanted to believe. Alas, I usually spent the entire evening without hearing from that Carmen or Roméo a single note well sung or word enunciated as it should have been. Occasionally, the performance is satisfactory, the lingering impression is pleasant, all the appearances of genuine singing are there—but a connoisseur will not be duped; and, formerly, two-thirds of the people in a hall were connoisseurs and knew after only a few notes how to assess the voice they were hearing.

So far, I have spoken only about the voice and vocal technique, leaving everything related to style, diction and expression still to be considered. These will be the topics of future lectures. Now, let us talk no more about the decline of singing. Let us try to forget it; for the time will come, after we have considered these other topics, to ask ourselves whether the esthetics of today's singers are really to our liking.

At present, I repeat, the competence of the public in general and of young people in particular lies in areas totally removed from music. You will find very few teenagers who cannot talk knowledgeably about the make, year and distinguishing characteristics of a certain car; they wax eloquent on the subject of airplane engines or boxing matches; on all those matters, one cannot "stump" them, they cannot be deceived. But take them to a performance at the Opéra or the Opéra-Comique, and you will see them placidly accept whatever vocal merchandise is currently peddled—merchandise that adolescents of former times would have rejected with disdain. In this case, why should anyone be embarrassed to offer third-rate musical fare? Believe me, in large measure, this is the root of the problem.

[1] ["*Chant*" ("singing") and "*champs*" ("fields") are homonymous; "*à travers,*" of course, is "across."]

[2] [Gustave Moreau (1826–1898), the noted Symbolist painter, had a great influence on Matisse. A museum in Paris is devoted to his paintings.]

³ [From Agathe's aria from *Der Freischütz* (1821), by Carl Maria von Weber.]

⁴ [From Joseph's aria from *Joseph en Egypte* (1807); by Etienne Méhul.]

⁵ [*Ibid.*]

⁶ [From Norma's prayer in *Norma* (1831), by Vincenzo Bellini.]

⁷ [*Ibid.*]

⁸ At recent competitions, I have seen definite progress in this respect, especially among male students. It seems they have finally concluded that the mere possession of a promising voice is not everything (August, 1920).

⁹ [Giovanni Mario (1810–1883), tenor, was a great favorite at the Paris Opéra for many years.]

¹⁰ [Erminia Frezzolini (1818–1884), soprano, sang with great success in Italy, France, Austria and England.]

VII

Expressive Singing in Early Music

Mesdames, Mesdemoiselles, Messieurs,

In our meetings to this point, we have established some sweeping principles of singing. Now we must move closer to our subject to examine in minute detail what we have already considered in its broad outlines as a part of the whole. First, allow me to remind you of a principle that I stressed at our very first meeting, which can be summarized as follows: Expression is inseparable from mechanics or technique; diction and singing are indissolubly united, for the expressive quality and the sound quality depend on each other; it is impossible to enunciate well and sing badly. The sound borrows its character or beauty from the words that give it form; the slightest shift of emphasis in the expression or meaning of the words will modify the sound; and, similarly, the sound, by its tone quality or volume, will change the meaning or the expressive effects of a word. Recently I had the occasion, twice in the same day, to verify these notions.

In the morning, I was with Doctor Wicart,[1] who, as you know, understands the larynx as if he had invented it. We were talking about physiology, vocal mechanism, and he described the workings of the vocal cords in a particular case. I responded, he responded to my response, and we were rapidly drawn into an extended analysis of certain intricate questions of psychology and expression. It turned out to be impossible to identify a specific mechanical process resulting in a specific sonority without observing that, for the expression of some particular mood, that sonority was inadequate. Moreover, it became clear that in order to continue in any particular vocal technique or position, it would sometimes be necessary to find a compromise between a sound and a word that conflicted with each other. However, in order to overcome this incompatibility of the sound and the word that the sound was voicing, it was necessary to adjust the feeling that inspired the mood to be expressed. To justify this tampering with the essential feeling involved, we had to go still farther and in some way alter or reinterpret the fundamental psychological concepts underlying the entire passage. Then, to justify this alteration, it was necessary to modify the original image of the character in question, down to the details of his or her appearance. And thus our discussion, which had started with a question about a resonant vibration, a purely physical phenomenon, slipped into the abstract spheres of psychology and even metaphysics!

The same evening I had dinner with my famous friend, the singer M. Jean de Reszke. We were alone, so, naturally, we ended up talking about the theater. Interestingly enough, our talk proved to be the mirror image of the morning's long discussion, a verification of the same points through opposite arguments. We began by talking about different ways to obtain a psychological understanding of a given role and to interpret certain scenes—the appropriate attitudes of mind, styles of diction, qualities of tone. Our conversation, gradually moving in the opposite direction from the one pursued earlier, became totally technical. We started by

Maria Garcia Malibran, Spanish mezzo-contralto
(1808–1836). Lithograph by Léon Viardot, 1851.

dealing with emotions and concluded by discussing strokes of the glottis and other purely physical matters.

Thus it must be understood that when I speak here of interpretation, of diction, when I emphasize an inflection, an emotional intonation, I imply a mechanical operation. I remind you of this so that you will not conclude that correct enunciation guarantees a good singing performance. You must constantly remember that the slightest expressive detail, superbly executed, is a small physiological tour-de-force.

Emotion and intelligence are always, in some proportion, required in a work of art. The chief requirement for singing is that it should be governed by appropriate feeling and insight. If we wish to convey an emotion, we must, first, experience that emotion, or imagine that we experience it, *precisely*. If we intend to suggest an image, we must, first, hold it in our mind, and it must faithfully reproduce the image that the composer held in his mind when he created what we now seek to interpret.

Today, let us talk about emotion in singing.

I am often amazed by the contrast I notice between the words uttered by a singer and the expression he gives them. That difference is not always due to lack of understanding. Fortunately, not all singers are like the one who gave the memorable answer to a question about Escamillo's aria. One day, as this singer was rehearsing the role of Escamillo in *Carmen,* M. Carvalho[2] was struck by the ferocious attitude he assumed as he sang:

Et songe, en combattant, qu'un oeil noir te regarde.

And think, as you fight, that dark eyes are watching you.

"But why," he asked the singer, "do you look so fierce when you sing *"qu'un oeil noir te regarde"*?

"To imitate the look of the bull," he explained.

What is most remarkable about the naïveté of this answer is not what is most obvious. Of course, to confuse the dark eyes of a lovely woman with the eyes of a bull is, in itself, quite mindless; but more surprising still is the fact that, in order to suggest the eyes of a furious animal, the singer *assumed a vicious expression.* In fact, to allude to a bull is not to imitate a bull, just as, to warn someone against a danger, we do not *imitate the danger.* If we say to someone coming down a stairway: "Watch out, you are going to fall," we do not feel compelled to tumble down ourselves to demonstrate the unpleasant effects of such an accident. Indeed, we should note in passing, the singer should generally refrain from excessive nuance, expression, mimicry and modes of diction.

It is not uncommon, in a scene or a portion of a scene, for a singer to interpret the feelings or repeat the words of another character, in which case one should exercise great caution. If, for example, one quotes words one was told, it is not always necessary to change voices and imitate the voice of the interlocutor. For instance, in the dream of Athalie,[3] it would be ridiculous to imitate the voice of Jezebel. By adopting a slight change in timbre, one may indicate that it is Jezebel who speaks; but Athalie, still trembling after her terrifying dream, could hardly be expected to give imitations. Further, assuming that Jezebel's own voice would reveal the ravages of time, we can see that it would be most unwise for Athalie to imitate it, adopting an old and shaking voice to exclaim:

Le cruel dieu des juifs l'emporte aussi sur toi!

The cruel god of the Jews also prevails over you!

It would be equally ridiculous, in the scene from Massenet's *Le Cid,* to hear Chimène, moved by her recollection of Rodrigue, trying to imitate his voice when she reminisces:

> *Il me disait, avec son doux sourire:*
> *"Tu ne saurais jamais conduire*
> *Qu'aux chemins glorieux et qu'aux sentiers bénis."*

> He told me, with his tender smile:
> "You would only know how to lead
> To glorious ways and to blessed paths."

Here Massenet was quite aware of possible awkwardness, for he has Chimène's phrase, on the contrary, flow smoothly and continuously. In fact, at this moment, as Chimène remembers and repeats those precious words, I would have her seized with fresh pangs of emotion, so that she is all but sobbing by the end of the phrase. At that moment, she is in the spotlight, she is at center-stage, and her father's words interest us only because of the grief they summon to her heart.

Often the words of one or several characters may be in opposition, yet the prevailing mood is unchanged. An example can be found in this dialogue from Gounod's *Roméo et Juliette.*

> *Ah! ne fuis pas encore;*
> *Laisse ma main s'oublier dans ta main.*

> Ah! do not flee so soon;
> Let my hand linger in your hand.

But Juliette, frightened by the first rays of dawn, answers:

> *Ah! l'on peut nous surprendre.*
> *Laisse ma main s'échapper de ta main.*

> Ah! one may discover us;
> Let my hand escape from your hand.

These two speeches move in opposite directions, yet the same music encompasses them both. Moreover, this sameness, far from being an oversight, is a very clever idea; for there is no doubt that, even as Juliette's fear, prudence and modesty make her want to leave Roméo, she wants to remain with him. And so she murmurs, "*Ah! l'on peut nous surprendre,*" with a tender, almost pleading tone, without urgency or conviction. The atmosphere of tenderness and love surrounding the young couple remains intact; thus it is appropriate that the music does not change. Indeed, it would be deplorable if the artist interpreting the role of Juliette sang her line in an agitated, imperious way.

Iphigénie en Tauride has a scene which gave rise to a well-known anecdote. Orestes, tortured with remorse, is pursued by the Eumenides. Following a long outpouring of grief, during which the violas, through panting, hammering syncopations, express the storm of confusion in his heart, Orestes believes that relief is near. He collapses, exhausted, and says:

> *Le calme rentre dans mon coeur.*
> Calm returns to my heart.

During a rehearsal of this scene, someone was surprised to hear the violas still frantically beating out their syncopations and said to Gluck: "How is it that he says calm returns to his heart, yet the orchestra continues with such agitation?"

Gluck replied: "He *believes* that calm is returning to his heart; but he has killed his mother, and he will never find peace again."

Tragic emotion demands such contradictions; and the singer must know how to use them as a fount of inspiration.

Now I would like to draw your attention to a special sort of citation that one encounters in singing. Occasionally, onstage, a letter is read aloud. In *Zémire et Azor,* by Grétry, one of the characters writes a letter and recites its text at the same time, with the result that the performer and the letter are on the same expressive plane, operating as one. But such is not the case when Charlotte reads Werther's letters: Charlotte is in a state of agitation, of anguish; here the difficulty lies in the fact that even in this distressed state, she must to able to read these letters in a way that reflects the passionate intensity of Werther, who wrote them, and, at the same time, to maintain a tone of voice that is flat and subdued, which is essential to convey the impression of reading. This is a very difficult feat indeed, which no doubt explains why singers rarely succeed in this scene.

We have strayed at some length in this discussion of conflicts that are sometimes necessary between the feelings to be conveyed and the words that convey them. Let us return now to our principal subject and concentrate on what is the more common, the more natural situation, that is, the rapport and harmony that usually exist between the words and the feelings they make manifest, between the state of the soul and the manner in which we express it.

I have already mentioned that I am frequently astonished by the difference, the contradiction, between the expression of some singers and the words they pronounce, and I added that this divergence could not always be attributed to a lack of intelligence. Very frequently, a manner of tone production which may be less faulty than awkward will modify and alter the meaning of an exclamation, a monologue or even an entire scene. In Gluck's *Alceste,* the High Priest, after consulting the oracle, announces that the king is doomed to death, but that he can be saved if someone else consents to die in his stead. Queen Alceste, in a sublime outpouring of love, declares that she is ready to die. The High Priest urges her to carry out her heroic sacrifice courageously and tells her that the ministers of death will meet her at the gates of Hades. She replies, "I will fly to accomplish a duty which is dear to me":

J'y volerai remplir· un devoir qui m'est cher.

Most singers, concerned about their voice, tend to "darken" the timbre during this phrase in order to enhance its sonority. But since the phrase lies in a rather high register and since the darkening of timbre can only be achieved by compromising strength and vivacity, the result is that this phrase is uttered gravely, with solemnity, instead of with the ardent, impetuous force of love which moves the queen to this stirring sacrifice.

For another example of the importance of choosing the right timbre, I refer you to Pylades' aria in Gluck's *Iphigénie en Tauride*. Orestes, who has murdered his mother and is now pursued by the furious Eumenides, arrives in Tauris, where a cruel cult requires that all foreigners must be sacrificed on the altar of the goddess Diana. Orestes, already overcome with sorrow and remorse, is further distressed by the thought that his faithful companion, Pylades, will have to die because of him. He expresses his emotions to Pylades in vehement words, but Pylades answers with deep affection and generosity. Here is the text of his recitative:

> *Quel langage accablant pour un ami qui t'aime!*
> *Reviens à toi, mourons dignes de nous;*
> *Cesse, dans ta fureur extrême,*
> *D'outrager et les dieux, et Pylade, et toi-même.*
> *Si le trépas nous est inévitable,*
> *Quelle vaine terreur te fait pâlir pour moi?*
> *Je ne suis pas si misérable,*
> *Puis qu'enfin je meurs près de toi.*

What grievous language for a friend who loves you!
Come to yourself, let us face a death worthy of us;
In your great rage, cease

To offend the gods, Pylades, and yourself.
If our death is inevitable,
What vain terror makes you tremble for me?
I am not so miserable,
Since, in the end, I die at your side.

These words both virile and tender are well chosen to encourage Orestes to take heart. I have no idea why one generally sings them in a plaintive way; it seems to me, on the contrary, that an almost cheerful vigor is required. Pylades wishes to console Orestes for having brought him so near to death, though quite unwillingly; but at the same time, he insists that his friend should die courageously, with no sign of weakness or anxiety, and that he should show himself worthy of his noble blood—the same blood which flows in his own veins, since Pylades and Orestes are cousins. Both men are the sons of kings, and Pylades is appalled by the thought that Orestes might revolt and face death with violence and cursing rather than with a supreme disdain. Equally strongly, he wishes to console Orestes for having been the cause of his death and to convince him that he is glad to die with him. This excerpt, though sometimes sung with emotion, is always sung too sadly; as I have said, a robust "cheer" should be added.

Moreover, although this scene does not lie in a particularly difficult voice range, tenors, in order to achieve a highly melodic style, instinctively resort to an uncomfortable means of tone production that tends, in fact, to produce a fleshy, plump singing line—a means that consists in favoring the vowel-sound *u* [as in the German *ü* or umlaut] while slightly tightening the throat. The first impression, even if the tone has a guttural quality, is pleasant enough; but soon the singer feels fatigue, for as the vocal line moves to a higher register, the position on the *u* becomes difficult. The listener is soon aware of this difficulty, which becomes more obvious as the aria continues.

This manner of tone production also gives the singing an affected quality; the pleasing sense of spontaneity disappears.

Orestes thus faces a Pylades who seems to be reciting a memorized statement in an artificial way. Actually, Pylades is expressing his joy in dying at his friend's side. It seems to me that in order to convey such a generous, heroic sentiment, more is required than a well-produced tone. A warm, convincing, almost joyful sound is essential here. The listener must understand Pylades' deep desire to convince Orestes that he rejoices in sharing his fate. Thus it becomes necessary to choose a vowel-sound other than *u* for the prevailing tone color—the vowel-sound *e* [as in *the* before a consonant], for example. What the tone may lose in fullness, in mellowness, it will gain in vitality and expression. At any rate, the best approach is to sing the aria with its *meaning* firmly in mind. Then, quite naturally, the voice will find its proper place.

There are many dramatic situations in which one must sing while appearing to cry. But there are different ways of crying; let us examine three quite different cases.

In the short melody by Pergolesi[4] that I will sing for you, one must have the impression that the eyes are brimming with tears but not yet overflowing. In one or two places, one must let them affect the voice. The hero of this simple, sad song is prey to continuing grief, for he says: "My disconsolate soul would accept an even crueler pain if, at least, it had the hope of one day knowing consolation."

Here we are dealing with a chronically grieving heart, so there is little likelihood that this lovelorn lad will cry each time he speaks of it! Furthermore, his plight may be only a shallow emotion, one of those gallant, fashionable despairs so frequent in 18th-century music which Pergolesi, a young man and a Neapolitan to boot, tends to exaggerate.

*   *   *   *   *   *   *   *   *   *

Let us see now how tears, real tears that well up in the heart and the eyes, can be expressed in singing. You are about to hear the ballad of Maître Wolfram, in which one must cry in earnest. Maître Wolfram finds solace in his tears and lets them flow abundantly. His grief is simple and heartfelt, never self-pitying, but resigned and candidly poured out in real tears.

You perhaps noticed that in the Pergolesi melody I just sang, I used a muffled, slightly strained timbre. In the case of Maître Wolfram, a character whose suffering is deeply inward, his grief must be expressed with restraint. I therefore modify my tone production by resorting to a sort of "interior yawning," adapting most of my pronunciation to the coloring of the vowel-sound *ou* [as in *choose*], which covers and dampens the sound. While pronouncing each word distinctly, I shall avoid an articulation that is projected forward, in order to reflect the deeply internal nature of the feeling. Moreover, towards the end of the selection, I shall not be afraid to add a bit of realism through the use of a kind of vibrato, similar to that obtained from string instruments and often used in early vocal music. In addition, I shall interrupt the *legato* line of the sound rather frequently.

* * * * * * * * *

Totally different still are the tears of Zurga in Bizet's *Les Pêcheurs de Perles* (*The Pearl Fishers*). These are tears of grief and remorse, but also tears of the Orient, which is to say, tears of pride. Zurga not only suffers from the loss of his friend and the loss of his beloved, he also suffers because he has capitulated to his own rage and jealousy. Perhaps, as a true man of the East, Zurga (to use M. Claudel's expression) fears celestial punishment. His despair is no doubt sincere, but it is mixed with egotism and tinged with grandiloquence and verbosity. Anyone who has seen Eastern displays of feeling, with much hair-tearing and chest-striking, will agree that it is correct to interpret Zurga's aria with a sort of nervous exasperation in which one senses that the tears are infinitely less simple and natural, less abundant, than in the case of good Maître Wolfram. Here, it seems that the tears emerge with difficulty, that they flow more from the voice than from the heart. With this passionate Hindu, they could only pour forth well adorned with lamentations and exclamations. Zurga is a powerful man, robust, in the prime of manhood; I can see him standing before me: his skin tanned, his eyes clear, his brow fierce and teeth gleaming, his nervous hands, decorated with glittering rings, pressing against his chest. What is needed here is a ringing, intense timbre; and so we shall choose the vowel-sound *o* as a general color for the tone—the short *o*, as in *botte* [or as in *mother*], the very sound suggested by Fauré for singing exercises (but which I would not recommend for everyone).

You no doubt realize, Mesdemoiselles, that what I am advocating here is nothing other than freedom in singing. Nietzsche said: "It is indispensable *to have a buoyant mind*," meaning a mind that assimilates and adapts easily. If this buoyant mind is necessary in philosophy, it is even more so in an art as changeable and impalpable as singing, in a singing career where one is obliged to pass through metamorphosis after metamorphosis in role after role. I am not an adherent of any one singing method, but I subscribe to all methods insofar as each serves a particular goal, one among the many we propose for ourselves.

If voice teachers were not, for the most part, more than a little vain, they would endorse this point of view. It is an everyday occurrence that artists who admire each other express diametrically opposed views about the art and the methods of singing. What does this prove if not the immense variety of approaches available to singers? Believe me, one must have a vast store of knowledge, borrow from every singing method, understand them all, have recourse to even the most discredited technique so long as the effect is desirable. Why forbid strokes of the glottis if they sometimes produce favorable results, adding life and strength to the word or the voice? Why use them constantly if they cause injury and strain? Why ban *portamento* if it can be used to create an elegant phrase? But why use it all the time if the results are sometimes vulgar? Why prohibit certain ways of breathing when each can serve a specific purpose and aid in the expression of a specific thought?

In truth, the singer must understand and employ all approaches, must know how to sing with or without strokes of the glottis, must know how to sing *legato* and *staccato,* how to produce a dark or a bright tone, how to produce a nasal tone and even a guttural tone. (Fauré, for instance, used a guttural tone for the high D, E-flat and E-natural.) One must know how to breathe from the chest, from the abdomen, through the nose and through the mouth; one must know how to breathe in every possible way and also how to limit one's breathing. To be the master of his craft, the singer must be aware of everything and disregard nothing of which the vocal apparatus is capable. But it takes time to attain such mastery, and we should not expect a student graduating from the Conservatoire to fully grasp the art and science of singing.

Mme Lilli Lehmann's treatise on singing contains the following remark: "Without counting the time required to learn the correct placement of the vowels, one should not hope to know how to sing before six years of constant studies."

Six years, eight years of studies she states elsewhere, and this does not include the progress we make every day of our lives, if we truly love singing. But rather than heed this sage advice, young singers, as soon as they have graduated, seek a contract from the Opéra or the Opéra-Comique, for they disdain provincial opera companies, which is a great mistake. Provincial companies offer an excellent training ground, where one can make enormous progress. Audiences in the provinces, more tight-fisted than

Parisians when it comes to money matters, tolerate no nonsense. Less excitable, less distracted by a thousand worries and temptations, the provincial public listens to music far more seriously than Parisian audiences do; so a singer making a debut in the provincial cities and anxious to establish himself cannot afford to undertake his task lightly.

For this reason, I can never recommend too strongly that singers should spend two or three years working with provincial opera companies before they make their debut in Paris. In so doing, they not only gain experience and hone their talents, but they also acquire that vocal stamina which is generally lacking in students when they emerge, worn out with working and still quite young, from the Conservatoire. But they are impatient to make a name for themselves in Paris and unafraid to sing at the Opéra-Comique or, still more disastrous, at the Opéra, where the acoustics pose formidable risks for inexperienced singers. For these beginners, the merest hint of success reinforces their natural vanity, which seems to be inseparable from vocal talent. From this moment forward, they believe they have nothing more to learn; so they give up forever the intellectual curiosity that every real singer should exhibit to the end of his or her life.

I recently found in the *Souvenirs* of Legouvé[5] an anecdote which supports my view that one must never stop thinking about singing.

> Mme Malibran had a mezzo-soprano voice, a voice which, as you know, is between contralto and soprano. Well, a warlike king, wedged in between two foreign kingdoms, could not have been more tormented by the desire to invade the lands of his two neighbors than was the great Malibran by her desire to cross over into the registers of the two bordering voices. What a surprise we had when one day she performed a trill on the highest soprano note. We were filled with admiration.
>
> "You are surprised?" she asked, laughing. "Oh, that cursed note! What trouble it has given me: For an entire

month now, I have been looking for it, while I dressed, while I combed my hair, while I walked, while I rode horses. This morning, at last, as I was putting on my shoes, I found it!"

"And where did you find it, Madame?"

"Here," she said, still laughing. And with a charming gesture, she touched her forehead.

Here, however, I must dilute the effect of this little story by taking a technical view of it. It is possible that Mme Malibran merely meant to point to the center of resonance for the particular note. But whatever her intention, it is a fact that Mme Malibran, at the zenith of a glorious career, was still hard at work in the pursuit of her art.

Our young artists not only refuse to apply mental effort to singing, they neglect their intellectual life in general. Alas, there is so much to be said on this matter! You can hardly imagine the ignorance and carelessness one encounters in most singers. Numerous examples come to my mind, but I shall mention only one.

Several years ago, a young soprano student at the Conservatoire told me that she planned to sing the last scene of Saint-Saëns' *Henry VIII* for her graduation exam in opera. I thought it was a good idea, and since I had for years accompanied Mme Krauss at the piano in that particular scene, which she performed admirably, I was sure this young lady would be interested in a description of the great artist's interpretation of the scene. Upon hearing the name Mme Krauss, she said: "Madame who?"

I was taken aback but not discouraged, so I continued to talk to her about the scene and the preceding acts. Dumbfounded, I soon realized that she had not the faintest idea of what had transpired in the opera before that final scene: the characters, the unfolding of the intrigue, the plot in general, were totally unknown to her. She had chosen this scene for her exam because one of her colleagues had succeeded in the exam with it, and that was all she cared about.

I insist that a singer must remain ever alert, ever inquisitive, never complacent but always restlessly searching for ways to give more and more meaning to a role, to a selection, even if he has performed it a hundred times. I insist that, in his solitude, the singer must think about the character he is to portray, must picture him as if he stood before him, must explore the depths of his soul. I insist that he must do his utmost to draw all that is deeply, intimately human from the music he performs. A singer who fails in this attempt does not interest me; but if he makes a fitting effort, even if he fails, I am on his side, I consider him a brother at heart. To me he is a kindred soul and fellow artist, and I offer him breathless attention and complete good will.

Some singers, when they appear onstage if only to say a few words, immediately command the audience's attention and preserve it even in the presence of other, more famous and exciting artists on the same stage. Two years ago, M. Vanni Marcoux was singing the role of the old Hebrew in *Samson et Dalila* at the Paris Opéra. This character has only a few bars, a few lines, to sing; but as soon as M. Marcoux came on the scene, everyone forgot about Samson and Dalila. His appearance, his acting, his slightest inflections were such that this simple "old Hebrew," this bit player who utters but a few words, became the personification of the Jewish nation persecuted by the Philistines. Thanks to the magical spell of this great artist, the audience was carried back to the roots of Jewish culture. All the Old Testament appeared, savage and grim, majestic, vast, gleaming with color and teeming with life. Since then I have heard other "old Hebrews," but in comparison, they were grinding bores.

I believe—and I hope you will agree—that it would be a good idea to set up at the Conservatoire, not a class in dramatic literature, which already exists and provides its teacher with the opportunity to relish, twice a week, what the poet Moréas calls "the bitter delights of solitude," but a less pretentious and more practical class, where young men and women, like children, would be taught matters of which they have no knowledge and which they would never learn elsewhere—where one would be treated to a smattering of history along with a wealth of anecdotes, many gossipy, amusing stories, details about the dress and manners of different ages. Such a class would be a treasure. Perhaps it would stimulate curiosity, and curiosity, once aroused, would stimulate a taste for work, for reading and literature, of which most of them know nothing. When they come to appreciate beautiful prose and fine verse, they will read more, they will even read aloud. And reading and contemplation can only have good effects. They will introduce young singers to a whole world of poetry, a picturesque world of imagination and feeling which they never knew existed. They will familiarize them with possibilities of clarity, balance and fluency in language, which can only enhance their singing. Who knows—they might become intelligent singers!

I believe too that from the very beginning of their studies, singers should be encouraged to sing in Italian. Italy has played a vital role in the formation of our vocal culture, and the Italian language is itself a form of singing. The musical aspect of this language is made even more pronounced by the spoken inflections brought to it by the Italians, this most expressive and melodious people. Italy, in a sense, was the cradle of modern singing, and it has produced many admirable singers. Italian music is a fertile source of material for singers, and the musical literature of this country offers much of value for their training and progress. Furthermore, the Italian language offers many opportunities to sing open vowels, which, as I have often noted, is of prime importance in singing.

Let me make a few closing remarks. I have been rather hard

on French singers, but I also believe that present-day Italian singers bear very slight resemblance to Italian singers of former times. As far as I know, and according to everything I have read, the latter pursued a totally different concept of singing: They avoided "strained" guttural tones and resonance produced under the tongue by extending the lower jaw; they did not stoop to cheap tricks or attempt to extract applause from the audience as one might extract a tooth.

If the French set their minds to it, they could be the best singers in the world.

---

[1] [Dr. A. Wicart, French laryngologist, wrote Le Chanteur (The Singer) in two volumes, with a foreword written by Reynaldo Hahn.]

[2] [Léon Carvalho, director and conductor at the Opéra-Comique, responsible for a poorly received revival of Carmen in 1882.]

[3] [Athalie, a drama by Racine (1691).]

[4] ["Una pena più spietata" ("A sorrow more merciless").]

[5] [Legouvé (1807–1903) wrote the play Adrienne Lecouvreur.]

Vanni Marcoux, French bass-baritone (1877–1962), in the title role of Mozart's *Don Giovanni*. Courtesy Photo Archive of Benedikt & Salmon Record Rarities, San Diego.

VIII

Evocative Singing

Mesdames, Mesdemoiselles, Messieurs,

At our last meeting, we came to the conclusion that in order to convey an emotion or project an image, a singer had, first of all, to be pervaded with that emotion to a point where he could feel it so deeply that, consciously or unconsciously, he would color and shape his voice according to its demands; or, in the case of an image, he had to hold it before his eyes at the very moment he described it. We even performed a few highly emotional selections as examples and looked closely at various methods of expression. Today, we shall consider what I call *evocative singing,* or, rather, *visionary singing,* and the principal ways to bring it about.

Throughout the ages, the object of music has been to describe, to evoke. Its emotional purpose is quite obvious, and it is hardly surprising that music should be used to translate inner emotions since those same emotions lie at its source. Music has always sought to express and awaken feeling; genuine expression, coming from the heart, has always been the principal concern of musicians.

But music has a power that is even more mysterious than its ability to move us. This is the power to create images, to present, as in a mirror, things which had vanished from our mind's eye. What is even more surprising, music has the power to suggest to the imagination things that were unknown to it but that it recognizes all the same. The magic of music sometimes evokes them clearly, sometimes through a cloud of luminous haze. And here we have the natural functions of literary art, which explains and clarifies, and of the plastic arts, which reproduce objects exactly. Those objects, described in words or reproduced through painting or sculpture, often suggest, by association, objects other than those before our eyes, which is quite extraordinary, in fact, quite marvelous. That it should be possible, without drawing a single line or pronouncing a single word (for I refer here to instrumental music) and by the sole power of sound, to create new images or resuscitate those that were dead, and that these images should have all the coherence of dreams, all the inherent order of a sequence of thoughts—this is a great mystery which psychology and physiology may attempt to explain, but which will remain, despite all, impenetrable and sacred.

Yes, music possesses a power of incantation capable of transporting us beyond our own time and place. Of course, it has this effect only on the imaginative and sensitive mind, for there are people to whom music means nothing, absolutely nothing, and among these are some of the greatest of human minds. In his remarkable study *Les Idiots musicaux* (*Musical Idiots*), Dr Ingenièros confers this humiliating designation upon the great naturalist Cuvier, the equally great historian Macaulay and the famed Victor Hugo. For those afflicted by this infirmity, music is merely a pleasant noise—pleasant, that is, if it does not last too long. Obviously, these are not the sort of people I refer to when I say that, by its very nature, music evokes strange and wonderful realms and faraway visions.

If purely instrumental music, without the aid of the voice or words, can be descriptive or evocative, how much more so must it become when its magic combines with the power of words, for the very purpose of words is to present a detailed image. In some cases, words merely underline or accentuate what the music expresses by its own means, as, for example, at extremely lyrical moments where the music sweeps everything before it, or where the music alone expresses all or almost all that needs expression. In such moments, words merely serve as footnotes to the music. The same is true in other situations, but time is too short for me to enumerate them here.

Most often, it is the words that gave rise to the music, the words that gave it birth in the mind of the musician. The words suggested images to the composer, they awakened feelings in him, and these feelings and images in turn gave birth to a particular group of sounds. This group of sounds came to constitute the scene or the selection that the singer performs. It could be that the selection, even without the words, possesses the power of evocation, since it is suffused with the meaning of the words, since it exists only because of the words. But those generative words, heard at the same moment as the music they inspired, confer on the music an additional force, increase its descriptive power tenfold and, above all, make its meaning crystal-clear.

As an example, I offer a few lines of Donna Anna's recitative from *Don Giovanni* ("By struggling, wrestling, twisting, I freed myself from him"):

e.piegarmi   Da lui misciolse

Here the words, generators of the music we are hearing, legitimately play the leading role, directing the feelings and impressions of the listener. In the usual case, the sequence of mental events is as follows: The word and the sounds it has called forth are heard simultaneously, but the word takes effect in the mind of the listener a split second before the sound takes effect— the action of the word precedes that of the sound with a speed that eludes perception or control—the time of a lightning flash is much longer than this interval.

The meaning of a word has scarcely etched itself on the mind when the music, itself saturated with this meaning, touches the mind in its turn, completing, reinforcing, clarifying by musical means the overall significance of that word. The music will sometimes adjust, reduce or amplify the basic meaning of the word, adding connotations the word lacked in itself.

But what is the outcome if there is no exact correspondence between the music and the word to which it is so closely linked; if, for instance, that word, because of the way it is pronounced, acquires a different meaning, or if it is simply weakened? The accompanying music will lose its apparent rapport with the word, and as a result, the intimate tie between the two will be damaged or destroyed. And here you have the biological explanation, if you will, of the imperative that the singer adapt his or her diction with absolute faithfulness to the requirements of the combined sound and word.

If I were to do no more today than urge you to sing with

appropriate feeling—to sing "I Am Titania the Blond"[1] without weeping and to sing the lamentation of Orpheus without crisply accenting each word—you might well hold it against me, even though it is never bad or useless to repeat what is true. No, I did not come here simply to repeat some hackneyed rules, but to tell you something that is worth your attention.

By a certain mysterious process I cannot pretend to explain, diction is clearly and profoundly influenced by inner mental visions. If, in attempting to describe something, you proceed only by pronouncing words, without having before your eyes the most exact reproduction possible of that object, your evocation of that image will be incomplete or inadequate. Likewise, the singer must have a vision in his mind's eye of whatever it is he wishes to evoke if he is to succeed in impressing this image upon his audience. And he must have this inner vision at the very moment he is singing. It is not enough to have thought beforehand about what he is going to sing.

Dare I say it? In my opinion, and contrary to what is customarily recommended, the singer must not think too much about his performance in advance. The singer's preliminary preparation must focus on the physical aspects—that is, on the timbre in general, on how to approach a certain precarious note, how to breathe, how to overcome various vocal and musical difficulties. But all that is intangible in singing, all that is meant to evoke powerful illusions, all that constitutes its magnetic power, should not be subjected to too much thought before the moment of singing.

You do not want to cloud or diminish your vision before conveying it. That vision must, by now, have become second nature to you, because for entire days, for weeks and months, it has been present in your mind. Now, just before the performance, you should let it fade into the background. Then, at the very moment of singing, you should summon it abruptly to the forefront of your mind and focus on it for the space of a few seconds. Thus you create a kind of surprise for yourself, you add to your own state of exaltation and rouse your mind and spirits in a way that gives wondrous power to your singing.

Just as you are incapable of conveying emotion if you feel none yourself, you will not succeed in suggesting a vision, an image, if you do not have it before your eyes *at the moment of singing.* If the words you pronounce describe various images, those images must take shape on an imaginary screen before your eyes, and they will influence your delivery in diverse ways. Why does this happen? I do not know. No doubt it is a mental phenomenon comparable to the physical phenomenon used in the manufacture of perfumes. I refer here to the current of air that passes over the flowers, becomes saturated with their aroma and carries it to a substance specially prepared to absorb it. We might say that singing assumes the role of this airy go-between, and, after picking up an intangible image, carries it—reproducing it as if in a faithful mirror—to the mind of the listeners. Like any other fact whose proof depends on the agreement of individual perceptions, this marvel may be debated; but it exists without a doubt.

Indeed, the singer must be able to *visualize;* for him, words must be concentrated images which, entering his brain, disperse and create illusion. In many cases, this talent can substitute for culture, which explains how the singing and acting of certain artists may bear all the signs of refinement and intelligence while, in fact, these performers are ignorant and uncultured. But cultivating the mind can never be harmful to artists, and if they are already talented in the sense just described, additional instruction can only augment their ability to visualize. What is more, enhancing this ability through further instruction may be particularly useful since not everyone is able to see in a way that is sound and *beautiful:* The vision may be sound but unpolished; it may be sound but incomplete and merely approximate; it may be sound but dull or clumsy or lacking in artistic quality.

Two paintings that hang next to each other in the Louvre in Paris may be of interest in our present discussion. One is the famous painting of a skate, a ray-fish, by Chardin, the other one a still-life by Desportes—same period, same general style, even the same subject, since both paintings show a collection of foods.

Chardin's painting has the ability to enrapture. The most trivial objects, though represented with meticulous exactitude, are invested with a radiance that seems to emanate from their inmost nature. The center of the picture is occupied by the ray. A large, limp fish with open eyes and a hideous mouth, hanging from an iron nail, it sparkles with all the jewels of the heaven and the sea; its open entrails send out a thousand reflections of ruby and pearl, emitting an odor of fish and sea-water, promising a succulent feast to be prepared by an invisible cook. Here is bounty from the sea, delight for the eye, pleasure for the palate. A dark pitcher, covered with dust through which one discerns a golden wine, stands nearby, along with a scattering of oysters, some chives in a tin dish, a few shining carp, a skimmer, a wide, earthenware pan and a discreetly luxurious tablecloth with delicate blue trim. All these objects surround, accompany the central subject while opposing or superimposing their forms, their meaning and their varied colors. The whole is a gleaming, well-balanced ensemble, revealing a modest, well-ordered abundance, a satisfying activity, a simple and most agreeable interior scene. This painting, realistic as it is, is filled with poetry. But chief among its virtues are beauty of content and beauty in the use of light, as Diderot, the philosopher and art critic, described it so well.

In Desportes' painting, as in Chardin's, we find accuracy of drawing and color, good design and careful execution, all showing integrity and skill. But sadness and dullness define this painting. As we look at the objects in this tableau, nothing awakens in us: No idea of beauty, no thought, comes to us. Bought at the market, carefully laid out and conscientiously reproduced, those foods have served their purpose, which was to serve as model for a diligent but boring painter.

By analogy, a singer may deliver the words and music with exactitude, but the singing is commonplace if nothing arises in the mind of the listener.

If, as you sing, you are to evoke an 18th-century scene, perhaps a scene in the style of the painter Watteau, and if your vision of the scene is even slightly vulgar or common, you will succeed in evoking neither a painting by Watteau nor a poem by Verlaine. Your singing will not communicate that mood of poetry, that slight melancholy; it will not have those gradations of light and dark which lend such charm to the works of that painter and that poet. Your singing will have a crude, dry precision and a heaviness that are, in themselves, "anti-18th century," such as one finds in the works of poor painters and the poems of poor poets who have tried in vain to evoke that mannered, elegant period, with its charming libertinism, its discreet gaiety and veiled sadness.

I cannot begin to tell you the horror I felt when, one morning in August as I was walking in the park at Versailles in the raw, early light, there suddenly appeared before me the large van of a cinematographic company carrying the entire court of Louis XIV on their way to frolic near the Apollo pond. There was a dreadful Sun-King, a sullen Mlle de La Vallière, a Marie-Thérèse, a Molière, a Bossuet. They all wore clumsy wigs and heavy make-up, and they were suffering from the heat. Louis XIV was losing his nose; Mlle de La Vallière was complaining of a toothache, and the lackeys, whose stockings were drooping around their skinny calves, were eating croissants as they waited for the next "shoot."

All too often, the singing I hear brings to mind this sorry excuse of an evocation of the age of Louis XIV. The accessories are there, more or less; but what is missing is precisely that which evokes its soul, the image necessary to give an inner life to external appearances.

We cannot survey here the innumerable ways in which singing can describe or evoke, so let us examine only a few. First, we will consider two of the most simple and commonly used approaches.

The first consists in enumerating the objects in the setting we wish to suggest by naming every one of them. In Gounod's *mélodie* "Venise," for example, the lines from Musset say exactly what the listener must be led to picture:

> *Dans Venise la rouge*
> *Pas un bateau qui bouge,*
> *Pas un pêcheur dans l'eau,*
> *Pas un falot.*

> In Venice, the red city,
> Not a single boat moves,
> Not a single fisherman in the water,
> Not a single lantern.

It is clear that if someone does not know Venice, has not spent nights strolling through the city, sleeping on the floor of a gondola in the dark, narrow, silent canals, this person will find it difficult to imagine the mystery of that city asleep in the midst of its phantasmagoric charm. Here the singer's imagination might suggest a haze that blankets everything, so that he expresses nothing with undue force or suddenness. The singer must resist the temptation to increase the volume of sound on the words "*pêcheur dans l'eau*," which are written on an ascending melodic line, and he must pronounce "*Pas un falot*" with a sort of muffled yawn, dulling any possible brilliance in his voice.

> *La lune qui s'efface*
> *Couvre son front qui passe*

D'un nuage étoilé,
Demi voilé.
Tout se tait,

The moon which disappears
Covers its passing brow
With a star-studded cloud,
Half veiled.
All is silent,

But then beginning with the next lines:

fors les gardes
Aux longues hallebardes
Qui veillent aux créneaux
Des arsenaux.

except the guardsmen
With long halberds
Who watch at the battlements
Of the arsenals.

The tone color must suddenly change. It is useless to try to portray the guards with their long halberds vocally; this is impossible. But one can evoke the place where they stand, the setting of stone, marble, and upright lines. For this purpose, one should choose a slightly rigid, unmodulated tone (using the short vowelsound *o* [as in *or*], avoiding all nuances. One should breathe after *"hallebardes"* and then complete the phrase without another breath. The phrase must come to an end gradually, like weaker and weaker reflections on the smoothly metallic surface of the Grand Canal. Unless the singer is remarkably stupid, he will succeed in conveying those various images very clearly.

Another very frequent occurrence in evocative singing is a description of an event. Here the role of the interpreter is more complex; the challenge consists in capturing the movement of a series of actions, and, what is even more important, presenting these actions in the proper light, with the appropriate mixture of shadow and brightness, in high or low relief depending on the circumstances, as, for example, in the recitative immediately before Donna Anna's first aria in *Don Giovanni.* You will perhaps remember the situation in the opera. Donna Anna tells her fiancé Ottavio what took place in her father's palace the night he was murdered. Everything in that recitative must be expressed by the way she uses her voice and by her diction.

There are several reasons for this requirement. First of all, the setting is Spain towards the end of the 16th century, which already implies restrained behavior, especially in the case of this young woman of the higher nobility, trained to behave circumspectly and to abhor excessive gesticulation. Second, this recitative addressed to her fiancé takes place on the street; her state of mourning, her beauty, her noble birth, compel her to be discreet and to attract no attention from passers-by. Finally, she suspects that Don Giovanni is the murderer, and he has just left them; he could still be lurking in the neighboring streets; he could even be watching her as she tells her story. Thus she must speak in a low voice (I mean, of course, in the relatively low voice that stage conventions decree) and, above all, with as few gestures as possible.[2] So her tone of voice and her verbal expression must describe and express everything.

* * * * * * * * * *

There are other instances where the situation and mood are summed up by a single word which sets the general tone. Here the words give the singer almost no help in creating an image in the listener's mind. The words do not describe the appearance of things, but focus instead on conveying a feeling; thus the singer, as he pronounces the words, as he expresses the feeling, must maintain, unchanged, the atmosphere he has created at the very beginning. Take, for example, the word *automne* (autumn). There are all sorts of autumns.

Sometimes, as in Gabriel Fauré's *mélodie* "Automne," for example, we have a November autumn—dismal, tragic, dreary. Do you think it would be sufficient to sing those lines and that music sadly, however striking the music may be, to convey an exact and true impression of the composer's intent? No!—one must look and look again at that particular autumn; one must recall a stroll at dusk through leafless forests and, then, start that stroll anew in one's mind while singing; linger in a clearing, contemplate the shivering, grey reflection of the sky in the water of a pond, experience again all the sorrow of those gloomy moments that somehow also filled us with bittersweet pleasure and rediscover, if need be, a tear in some recess of our heart.

"But," one might reply, "I have never experienced such a moment at dusk in autumn."

Really? In that case, it would be best to give up singing altogether.

Now let us look at a fragment of the "Poème d'octobre."

Profitons bien des jours d'automne où, dans les cieux,
Semble errer la langueur plaintive des adieux.

Let us take advantage of autumn days when, in the skies,
The plaintive languor of parting seems to hover.

Here, a totally different vision must be communicated. It is the autumn of a poem by Lamartine:

Salut, bois couronnés d'un reste de verdure . . .
Greetings, forests crowned with a remnant of green . . .

There is still melancholy in this autumn, but there is also joy. The voice should not be supported as it was a moment ago, nor should it connect the sounds so closely, reflecting an unbroken span of grey clouds overhead. A slight sadness is needed here, and though the vocal delivery sometimes becomes more intense, it must immediately be veiled and subdued. Here we have the autumn of October.

Finally, we come to a third autumn, which is that of a lovely, little-known *mélodie* by Massenet: "Septembre," composed to the powerful verses of Hélène Vacaresco. This autumn is still warm and tender, bathed in the light, as Baudelaire said,

> *De l'arrière-saison, le rayon jaune et doux . . .*
> Of summer's end, the soft, yellow light . . .

This appealing landscape, still touched with color, reminds us of Mme de Sévigné's description of "those beautiful, crystal days which are no longer warm and not yet cold."

⁂

Every artistic performance involves practical details, and this leads me to speak of a matter that is very important (regardless of what others may think), a matter which plays a major role in artistic illusion. I am speaking of the singer's attitude.

Allow me to read a few memorable lines from Mme Lilli Lehmann's *Treatise on Singing:*

> Beginning with the very first note of the very first word, the artist must set the scene for his audience, giving them a sense, in advance, of its character. This is partly accomplished by the attitude he assumes as soon as the introduction begins, and also by his facial expression. Through his appearance, the singer can stimulate interest in what is to come, musically as well as poetically.

If we could look through the roofs of all the drawing-rooms, all the concert halls where singing is taking place in the course of a single evening, we would see that, among the hundreds of singers, not a single one observes this logical and useful rule. Why does a composer introduce a song with a prelude if not to lull or excite the listener into the appropriate frame of mind for what he is about to hear, to establish the proper background and mood for what he wishes to project? And the introduction has still another purpose: It inoculates the singer, so to speak, with the poetical virus that must spread throughout his body if he is to create, in a natural way, a particular impression. The singer can profit greatly from intense concentration during the few bars of the introduction: first, to bring the necessary feeling or setting into sharp focus; second, for the more mundane but equally important purpose of "settling down" vocally, if I may use that expression—to take a deep breath, to set his vocal apparatus, to swallow if necessary, to make sure that his larynx is clear and, on the very threshold of the mystery that is vocal music, to compose his thoughts about his performance. Finally, as Mme Lehmann noted, he can exert his personal magnetism for the space of several moments, through his attitude and his facial expression.

But instead, what do we see?

1. The singer who surveys the audience, looking for his friends.
2. The singer who, uncertain of his pitch, tries the note before beginning. This can occur in two ways: Either he sounds a wrong note and starts on it, or he sounds the right note but starts on a wrong one anyway.
3. The singer who, preoccupied with the details of his attire or thinking of other things altogether, completely forgets to sing at the end of the introduction and is abruptly recalled to reality by the anguished silence of the accompanist.
4. The singer who forgets to breathe before beginning to sing. He then compensates in one of two ways: He launches into the song without a breath, or he breathes at the very last moment and nearly chokes.

None of this is conducive to evocative singing. How can one expect the public to be in a receptive mood, to begin to visualize suitable images, if the mood is set in such a peculiar fashion.

Now let us assume that none of the above occurred or that in the course of the performance, the audience has forgotten the awkward beginning. Let us further assume that good communication was established between artist and audience, that the latter was affected and even moved by the former. The selection ends with a rather long postlude after the last bit of singing.

Alas, most singers, and especially female singers, through thoughtlessness, carelessness and, I would add, lack of respect for the composer, destroy the poetical or emotional effect they have achieved as soon as they have sung the last note. During the postlude, they fold up the music they are holding, smile, whisper something to the accompanist to appear important, and so forth and so on.

George Sand writes about Chopin:

> Sometimes, after having plunged his audience into a state of deep contemplation or acute sorrow (for his music, especially when he improvised, could cast a spell of utter dejection), suddenly, as if to erase the impression and memory of his pain, for his audience and for himself, he would turn furtively toward a mirror, rearrange his hair and his cravat, and then turn back to the audience transformed into a phlegmatic American, an impertinent old man, a sentimental Englishwoman, a Polish Jew.

Such off-handed behavior may sometimes be acceptable in a private setting; but even so, it must be entirely conscious, intentional, justified by the mischievous temperament or the stature of a talented performer. But such lack of ceremony should neither be permitted in practice nor accepted in principle, insofar as it abruptly terminates whatever mood has been created.

Let us return to the subject of specific evocations. It is not difficult to "compose" a vision inspired by Lalo's "Marine." The words and the music are extraordinarily descriptive; it is sufficient merely to follow them. And yet, in this selection, the singing and breathing must constantly remind us that ocean winds and breezes are blowing all around us. Diction and tone production that are too neat, too clear, too correct, weaken this impression of the open sea, prevent us from sensing the ocean spray in the air and the flight of the gulls soaring in the sky above. Actually, no sea spray, no gulls, are mentioned in these verses; I am responsible for adding them, and I apologize for this. But what can I do! Once creating a mental vision becomes a habit, one forgets where to stop.

* * * * * * * * * *

Fauré's "Le Cimetière" also mentions the ocean, but in an incidental way and only towards the middle of the *mélodie,* creating a contrast with the quiet cemetery where one rests in utter peace. I could not say why, but I feel the presence of the ocean throughout the selection, though this is never indicated. In my imagination, this rustic cemetery is near the sea. It seems to me that the sea provides a backdrop, and, perhaps for this reason, I imagine the scene in the wild, barren landscape of Brittany. The mourners attending this funeral are grave and pious peasants. All this combines in a vision that compels me to sing this *mélodie* without vibrato, in a resigned voice, with little color, little inflection, through which I hope to convey the simple, earnest, bare-bones dream of a Breton peasant.

* * * * * * * * * *

Earlier, in Gounod's "Venise," you saw a particular aspect of Venice: the secretive, nocturnal city with its small, dark canals, its murmuring waters, its roofs illuminated by moonlight, its mystery and its suggestive fragrance. In Fauré's "Barcarolle," you see another Venice, a more ethereal Venice, more joyful, more lively, the Venice of the *Riva degli Schiavoni* and the Rialto. One must convey this general impression through the coloration of the voice and the hammering of the consonants, by broad nuances, an open sound, a robust nonchalance in the pace . . . and so forth and so on.

[1] [Philine's aria in Ambroise Thomas's opera *Mignon*.]

[2] Needless to say, the end of the recitative requires warm lyricism and sonority, which is justified by the gathering intensity of her narration and her memory of the events.

Emma Calvé, French soprano (1858–1942), in the title role of Massenet's *Sapho*. Courtesy Photo Archive of Benedikt & Salmon Record Rarities, San Diego.

IX

About Taste

Mesdames, Mesdemoiselles, Messieurs,

When we met in this lecture hall after a three-month hiatus, I announced that I would not adhere to a definite plan, nor would I be confined by the titles announced for these four additional lectures. I further announced that I would proceed by stops and starts, lingering wherever caprice led me, as I explore the domain of singing; that I required freedom; that I would deal with the announced topics, but at my convenience and in whatever order I chose. However, what have I done after all? I have simply followed the program. My first lecture in the series was about the decline of singing. In the second, we spoke about expression; in the third, about various forms of evocative and descriptive singing; and today, after declaring that I would speak about whatever I fancied, I shall speak on the subject of *taste,* just as the flier announced.

Considering the subjects we have covered so far, I would find it logically impossible to conclude these lectures without dealing with the necessity and importance of taste. Indeed, in our meetings, I have repeatedly stressed that an able singer must possess and use, according to circumstances, all the resources of his or her art; must use them appropriately—whether to express a feeling or to evoke a setting or a particular object—and always with discernment and taste. In all my descriptions, I might have limited myself to a single word: *taste.*

For, when singing is not directed by the heart (and you know that one cannot lightly command the service of the heart), when singing is not guided by feeling, by understanding, by the direct outpourings of the heart, it is taste that assumes control, directing and presiding over everything. Then it must be everywhere at once, acting in a hundred different ways. Think of it! Every detail of the vocal offering must be submitted to the dictates of taste.

Let me be precise. By *taste,* I do not mean that superior and transcendent ability to comprehend what is beautiful which leads to good esthetic judgment. In fact, we cannot ask all singers to be people of superior taste, since such a requirement would reduce still further the very limited number of possible singers. By *taste,* I mean a wide-ranging instinct, a sure and rapid perception of even the smallest matters, a particular sensitivity of the spirit which prompts us to reject spontaneously whatever would appear as a blemish in a given context, would alter or weaken a feeling, distort a meaning, accentuate an error, run counter to the purposes of art.

I repeat: A particular sensitivity of the spirit is necessary in this sort of taste, as well as emotion and a certain fear of ridicule. It is no doubt for this reason that women display a better sense of taste in singing than men. I do not mean that women, in general, sing better than men, but that they sin against taste less frequently. They have the habit of attending to details of their appearance, they instinctively feel a desire to present themselves in the best light possible, they are skilled in a perpetual vigilance, a quick, sure instinct which watches over everything around them. For almost all women, glancing at themselves in a mirror is almost a reflex—a habit which has its advantages. In the same way, a singer must cultivate his or her taste by glancing habitually into an imaginary mirror and attending scrupulously to every detail in order to correct and improve his or her "vocal appearance."

Let us look now at some of the many ways in which taste in singing shows itself.

First, how can one choose what one will sing, what one *can* sing, without the assistance of taste? Here is a delicate question which cannot be answered logically. Consider the person with a large soprano voice, who is expected to sing the large soprano roles (the *lirico spinto* roles). But what if that person does not look the part? What if only her voice is consistent with the character of a large soprano role? I cite this situation because I recently had to deal with it.

A very tiny, truly diminutive person, a veritable sprite in a straw hat with a ribbon, appeared before me saying: "Ah! such stage fright! Oh! la, la! I have the worst case of stage fright!"

"Mademoiselle, what are you going to sing for me?"

"The aria of Dido in Carthage."[1]

Dido! Carthage! What formidable words! But they did not intimidate this small creature. She sang: Her voice was beautiful, ample beyond all proportion to her petite figure; that voice was her one great asset. But the overall impression was embarrassing, painful; the melodic stream came forth abundantly, pouring from that slender throat which seemed to be all larynx. And the expression? It was perfectly acceptable; it was conventional, but this aria by Piccinni is intrinsically so conventional that the lack of emotional force in the singer's interpretation was not offensive. Furthermore, this poor young woman took her performance very seriously: She sang with body and soul. What could I tell her? That her body and soul multiplied a thousand times would still not reach the measure of Dido's towering person? Why devastate this young woman who was so cheerful, so happy to have a beautiful voice? And yet, that particular voice in that particular body, that voice at the service of this little songbird: Was it not nature's mistake?

What has become of the diminutive lady with her straw hat? I never saw her again; but I can quite well imagine the many disappointments she has had to endure because of the contrast between her voice and her appearance and, most importantly, between her voice and her essential character—for this is where I wish to lead our discussion. Nature can permit itself liberties and mistakes that we humans dare not imitate. Thus I offer this advice: *Do not sing what you cannot properly feel, even if your voice seems to fit the part.*

I am less shocked by the frequent disparities between the selections performed and the voices performing them than by the complete incompatibility I often note between the particular composition and the singer's *personality*. I simply cannot comprehend the many teachers who show total disregard for the text and the meaning of the selections they give their students. Does it matter that this young baritone is ruddy-faced, roughhewn and plebeian? He will sing the aria of Henry III from *Le Roi malgré lui*[2] because his voice has the necessary range. Another young student is huge and timid. No matter! She will sing Cherubino's aria because someone has added a B-flat, *pianissimo,* to Mozart's aria, and this enormous demoiselle has a lovely *pianissimo* B-flat. This is utter lack of taste.

And here is another matter: dress etiquette. I won't dwell on this subject, but I would like to point out that women, especially, should choose clothing that conforms to the general style of what they are singing. I know this is not always easy, and that selections of very different kinds may be combined in a single concert. In this case, one should choose a neutral style of dress, suitable for everything. I can assure you that there is something quite unpleasant about hearing the poetry of Sapho[3] performed by someone wearing a hobble skirt.[4] This is an offense to taste.

Let us move on—but not before I mention a matter I overlooked during our last meeting, in our discussion of desirable stage deportment. An overly relaxed and graceless posture is as undesirable when singing as a tense and stiff posture. The former prevents the singer from keeping his or her voice well in hand, while the latter tends to alienate an audience and is an obstacle to variety of expression, to genuine singing.

The singer must try to avoid beating time with a foot, a knee, or even surreptitiously with a finger; believe me, it will always be noticed. Nor will beating time prevent mistakes if the singer is not secure in *solfeggio.*

But, how naïve of me to mention *solfeggio!* Does anyone pay attention to that any longer? Yes, I do mean *solfeggio!* Does anyone really believe in tying oneself down for a year or two to tackle the necessary studies? After all, the time spent on exercises is time that cannot be spent performing, and what comes first is proving that "one knows how to sing." A good sense of timing? Why worry about that?

Pardon me, but here I must interrupt. A good sense of timing, an understanding of rhythm, is, and I cannot repeat this often enough, the very first principle, *absolutely the first requirement,* of a good musical performance. One cannot impress or move an audience with vague, floating rhythms. It is not my intention to return to the subject of rhythm today; but I wish to insist that one of the mysterious virtues of rhythm is its ability to hold and fix the attention of the listeners so that they will miss none of the poetical and musical message. Rhythm is the pulse of music and its secret heartbeat. If it slows down, it is because the music moves at a slower pace; if it rushes forward, it is because the music intensifies. Music without rhythm is a body without muscles, weak and useless matter. To ignore rhythm is to display a serious lack of taste. This is equivalent to disregarding the laws of balance and proportion which are the elemental laws of all the arts.

cᴇ⅋ᴏ

A basic tenet of taste, in the most ordinary sense of the word, is tidiness, the absence of disarray. In fact, lack of rhythm is lack of taste because it is so untidy. Singing without rhythm is like an unbuttoned gown, a room in disorder, behavior that is rude or offensive. Without rhythm, the words that are sung lose their meaning. The audience understands less or understands incompletely. Then attention wanes; they become less responsive.

Music-hall singers (*chanteurs de café-concert*) almost universally have a good sense of rhythm. Because they appear on the popular stage, where the public is much more caught up in the spoken word than in the music, music-hall singers must know how to *project the words through the sound.* It is this that gives them such flexibility, that gives them the habit of endowing the sound with a great variety of nuances and expressions. Music-hall artists learn to transform the sound in all the ways the text requires. In order for the words to retain their force and to produce the required effect, one must observe the laws of rhythm; this is essential if the audience is to remain alert and receptive. This explains why music-hall artists sing so rhythmically—and also why serious singers (or those who pretend to be serious) should go often to listen to their more humble colleagues, for they provide some very useful examples.

I am sure you are aware that some music-hall singers were very remarkable artists; there are still a few. M. Polin is not merely a *diseur* [literally, one who "says" with art], a crooner. A singer who "croons" as he does, sings well. One has to have heard him perform one of his half-comical, half-sentimental *chansons* to realize what artistic intuition and taste can make of a little song, a ditty of no importance. But then, M. Polin has an admirable sense of rhythm. When he sings one of those *chansons* in which, with a good deal of mimicry and exaggerated breathing, he creates the impression of a marching regiment, a whole troop of soldiers sweating in heavy uniforms on a warm summer day and yet cheerfully enduring the many discomforts, one cannot help but admire his impeccable rhythm—invariable, relentless, always brisk, crisp and relaxed at the same time—and also the way in which this remarkable artist can work innumerable small inflections of diction into his steady, precise rhythm. Also admirable is M. Mayol's rhythmic precision, which forms the basis for a thousand piquant subtleties of gesture and diction.

Taste must guide performance in many other ways as well. For instance, it must give the singer an instant sense of the pace and the style that are right for a particular work. You may remember that, in my comments on style, I maintained there was no such thing as a single, unalterable style suitable for the entire range of vocal literature. Perhaps if we replace the word *style* with the word *taste,* the matter will be clearer. Taste tells a singer how to bring out the emotional character or the spirit of a composition, in keeping with the sensibilities of the period of its creation or, perhaps, the period of its revival. Singing an aria by Rameau as one sings a song by Schumann demonstrates a lack of taste; but it is equally tasteless to give the same interpretation to two *mélodies* written by the same composer on different themes. "Le Cimetière" and "Clair de Lune" were both written by Gabriel Fauré, but it should be clear to anyone who is not an imbecile that they cannot be sung in the same way. Among M. Fauré's compositions, there is a *mélodie* much closer to that very same "Clair de Lune"; this is the delightful "Arpège," which also describes a rural scene at dusk. A singer of average refinement (which does not mean a bad singer, but rather a typical one) could very well miss the differences taste requires in interpreting these two selections, for their similarities would mislead him.

Good taste will also guard us from the pitfalls of well-defined periods and specific musical genres. The following example should help to make my meaning clear; it is an excerpt from a cantata by Gervais,[5] "L'Amour vengé" ("Avenged Love"). A shepherd complains of the cruelty of a certain shepherdess and considers himself the most miserable of men. His confidant and friend, attempting to console him, tells him how to avoid the pangs of love. He says: "Am I fretting? Am I so foolish as to surrender my heart to these fickle shepherdesses? Do as I do. Take these 'passing amours' less seriously, and you will feel better." Common sense makes it clear that the interpretation here should be light, smiling and roguish—characteristics that exactly express the mood of the Regency era during which this sprightly music was written.

But what if I should wish to introduce some poetic feeling into this hare-brained fellow, this sceptic? What if I imagine that he has become so callous and jaded because he himself has suffered enormously as a victim of unhappy love? His wound has now healed; but he is prudent and will not expose himself again to such sorrow. Still, from time to time, memories come back against his will, and bitterness returns to his heart and his lips. Mind you, all this is the product of my own imagination; nothing, absolutely nothing in the text or music suggests these ideas. I have the absolute right to interpret this selection as I please. But what will prevent me from exaggerating, from going beyond what is proper, from totally distorting the song by injecting an overdose of sentiment? Taste will serve this function. Taste alone will tell me the exact degree of melancholy I can introduce into my singing, and the exact amount of time—which must be no more than a moment—I can devote to this small added nuance.

*   *   *   *   *   *   *   *   *   *

Taste governs many of the small details of singing; it has a bearing on a multitude of imperceptible elements which together determine mood or feeling. For instance, there are numerous small ornaments in the selection "L'Amour vengé." The signs used at the time to indicate how they were to be executed were very arbitrary and have produced considerable uncertainty as to their meaning. With some knowledge of early music, one can improvise as each situation may suggest. But I do not believe we can hope to precisely reproduce the manner of singing in former times. Indeed, I think we would all be dumbfounded if Mlle Lerochoy or the tenor Legros were to suddenly spring to life and sing before us. However, we can approximate the effect of early vocal ornamentation if we give the earlier era much thought and if we are willing to *enter into the spirit of that age* before we begin to sing. Again, it is a matter of taste.

Taste plays a key role in controlling the flow of breath, as does our sense of the feelings involved (for we must keep in mind that in singing, breathing is not merely a means of supplying oxygen to the singer's body).

In "Le Parfum impérissable," we saw that emotion or feeling primarily determines the manner of breathing. In other instances, breathing is governed by taste alone; in still other cases, taste and feeling combine to suggest a way of breathing that may be quite spontaneous, quite unusual. Taste is also a guarantee of moderation, in the expression of emotion as in vocal output. A man who possesses a beautiful voice but who, no matter what he sings, is chiefly concerned with showing off that voice, with dazzling the listener with that voice, shows a flagrant lack of taste. He will not, in deference to reason or logic, "sometimes put his voice in his pocket," as Gounod has advised; he must advertise his beautiful voice to all the world. He reminds us of the parvenu who emerged from the theater and called very loudly to his footman: "Bring up the master's coach!"

What does it matter if Don Giovanni is supposed to arrive quietly in the night, picking a mandolin, to serenade a lady's maid behind her curtains—this does not matter to our brazen singer with the beautiful voice: He bellows! An elementary sense of taste would prevent this insult to Mozart. Even in the "Brindisi" of *Hamlet*,[6] which is a selection requiring full voice, it is unnecessary to sing with thunderous noise. Of course, a singer needs a voice, even a large voice; but volume must always be moderated by taste. In some cases, taste may require a loud and powerful tone, a tremendous vocal display. But it is usually in the interests of moderation that taste must intervene.

[1] [From *Didon* (1783), an opera by Niccolo Piccinni.]

[2] [*Le Roi malgré lui* (1887): an opera by Emmanuel Chabrier.]

[3] [From *Sapho* (1850), Gounod's first opera.]

[4] This was written in 1914; today [1922], ladies' skirts are even less suited to Sapho's poetry.

[5] [Charles Gervais (1671–1744), French composer.]

[6] ["O vin, dissipe la tristesse," from Ambroise Thomas's opera *Hamlet* (1868).]

Conclusion

So, Mesdemoiselles, we have arrived at the end of our lecture series. There remain many things to be said on the subject of singing, for it is an inexhaustible topic, substantively and esthetically. I may someday have the good fortune to continue our conversation. Until then, I hope I have convinced you of certain truths which are precious to me, especially the following, which I cannot emphasize sufficiently:

Singing is beautiful only if it is meaningful. A beautiful voice, a strictly vocal performance, may provide a certain pleasure but cannot truly satisfy the listener, nor is it a form of art. Singing must affect us in a more than superficial way: It must address our mind and imagination and stir our deepest emotions. Such singing is a difficult task. A singer must acknowledge this challenge and take it to heart; then, through rigorous training, he or she must strive to acquire the technical mastery which will permit him to use his voice to serve his thoughts, his imagination and the stirrings of his heart. Finally, by constantly observing, contemplating and reflecting, he must imbue his singing with that expressive, dynamic and suggestive power without which singing has but little value.

Sybil Sanderson, American soprano (1865–1903), in the title role of Massenet's *Thäis*. Courtesy Photo Archive of Benedikt & Salmon Record Rarities, San Diego.

Further Thoughts on Singing

[Introductory remarks omitted here deal with the use of
recordings in teaching voice, particularly with the advantages of recording a student's singing and playing it back—
something quite new in the early 1940's but common today.]

The Uvular and the Rolled R

I received the following letter dealing with a matter that has
always interested me and particularly so of late, since I seem to
notice among young singers a tendency to use the uvular *r*, a
practice I have pointed out many times in my examination reports
following competitions at the Conservatoire and which I did not
notice among singers of only a short time ago. What surprises me
is the fact that, during the examinations and competitions, most of
the audience and even members of the jury do not seem particularly disturbed by this practice. Here is the letter, minus a few
details:

I read with keen interest your articles on music and singing appearing in *Le Figaro*. In a future article, at the appropriate time, I would like to ask you to treat the following topic: How does one pronounce the *r* in singing? In your comments on singing in the *Initiation à la Musique* (Editions du Tambourinaire), you state that, while singing, one must not use the uvular *r* (*grasseyer*). Thus, one must roll the *r*? Why?

Why? Because one has never heard a single great singer use the uvular *r* in singing serious, solemn, dramatic, delicate, poetical or sentimental music. Because the uvular *r*, which occurs in every-day speech in many regions of France, Germany and the Scandinavian countries, has a common, familiar sound, a prosaic and everyday character which contrasts with musical language. Because the rolled *r*, pronounced with the tip of the tongue, has always been required by the great singing teachers, not only the Italians (who, in fact, together with the Spanish, Orientals and Slavs, know no other way to pronounce the *r*), but also teachers in France and Germany. The rolled *r* is the most pleasant to the ear and the most conducive to good tone production.

I seem to recall that the distinguished singer Mme Louise Matha always rolled the *r* while singing; yet in an interesting account published by the *Revue Française de Phoniatrie* (*The French Journal of Phonetics*), she argues against that practice, which few singers and theorists of singing appear to have discussed. She supports her argument with a clever line of reasoning which may have theoretical value but which has not convinced me.

I myself cannot abide the uvular *r*; it gives me an impression of clumsiness, harshness and vulgarity. I am speaking, of course, of what we call serious music, for in operettas and *chansons* . . . but let me not get ahead of myself.

My correspondent continued:

Nothing is more difficult than the definition of phonetic matters. First, we must agree on the wording to use.

Experts on phonetics, we are told, distinguish among several ways of pronouncing the *r*: first, the Parisian *r*, used in everyday conversation in Paris; then, the rolled *r*, characterized by the fluttering of the tip of the tongue against the palate, the one used by almost all singers, which is abominable, in my opinion.

I omit the other *r*'s mentioned in the letter, for they only confuse our discussion. The following two suffice for our purposes: the Parisian *r*, which is altogether uvular (a "scraped" *r*, if you will), and the rolled *r*.

"Why should a detestable pronunciation in the spoken language"—the writer was referring to the rolled *r*—"be accepted in singing?"

Now it is my turn to say: Why? Why is it, Monsieur, that you find the rolled *r* so abominable? That *r* is natural for many French people. In subtly different ways, it is used by the natives of Touraine, Normandy, Burgundy and the Southwest. This *r* gave luminosity and cheer to the language of the troubadours; in the Pyrenees, it gives the language of the people the gentle murmur of a spring. I was recently in Toulouse, where my taxi driver spoke in such a delightful way, with rolled *r*'s so sparkling and yet so mild and sweet, that I made a long and costly detour simply for the pleasure of hearing him talk.

As for the rolled *r* of the Périgord, how can you fail to appreciate its rich and mellow sonority? No doubt, Monsieur, you have never heard Mounet-Sully, who never uttered an uvular *r* in his life (he would have been incapable of doing so, as would his brother Paul Mounet); but his rolled *r*'s had a multitude of nuances, from the most caressing softness to the most terrible violence. In fact, he very frequently used, as does M. Albert Lambert, the *vibrant r*, which is a sort of rolled *r*, as well as the truly uvular *r* (obtained by means of uvular vibrations against the lower part of the tongue, and rarely heard) which is an intensification of the Parisian *r*, the one we have called the "scraped" *r*. In singing, one must use the two lingual *r*'s, the rolled and the vibrant, depending upon the requirements of expression and taste.

Yet one must proceed with subtlety. Let us take two examples from Gluck's *Armide:* "*Ah, si la liberté me doit être ravie!*" ("Ah, if my liberty must be taken away!"). Here, shall we pronounce the three *r*'s in the same way? The one in "*liberté*" and the other in "*être*" must be simply rolled, while that in "*ravie*" must carry a light vibration. In fact, it would be nonsensical and unpleasing to sing: "*Ah, si la liberrté me doit êtrre . . .* , while in the word "*ravie,*" a simple rolled *r* would be weak and inadequate. In the duet in which Armide and Hidraot appeal to the demons and cry out: "*Esprits de haine et de rage!*" ("Spirits of hatred and rage!"), the *r* in "*Esprits*" must vibrate slightly, but the *r* in "*rage*" must vibrate very strongly in order to offset the effect of the very definitely aspirated *h* of "*haine*" and to emphasize the fierceness of expression.

My correspondent continued:

> I am not a singer; it is my delight in a beautiful performance that makes me hard to please, as is the case for all those who do not perform themselves. But I do notice that most music-hall singers, whose articulation is almost always perfect, never or rarely roll the *r*'s. If only for this reason, I can understand M. Tino Rossi's success. On the other hand, the admirable and well-controlled voice of Mme Ninon Vallin upsets me because of her exaggerated rolled *r*'s. At any rate, all the artists who have emerged from the Conservatoire have the same habit.

Dear Monsieur, there are many errors in your last paragraph. First of all, if indeed many music-hall singers (who are often worthy of admiration) use the uvular *r,* many others, including the most famous, roll the *r*'s. The distinguished Thérésa rolled them (in my youth, I had the good fortune of hearing her), the inimitable Paulus did the same, as did Mlle Duparc and, later, the unforgettable Polin. The variety of rolled and vibrant *r*'s employed by Mme Yvette Guilbert is staggering. M. Mayol rolls the r's; M. Georgius rolls the r's; M. Ouvrard, Jr., rolls the r's. I could name dozens more.

This said, I must add that the uvular r is perfectly acceptable in *chansons* and particularly in operettas, so long as the quality of diction and voice compensate for it. A case in point was Mme Simon Girard, who used the uvular r, but with a charm, a spirit and a talent for singing that compensated for anything. By contrast, Anna Judic and Mme Jeanne Granier never used the uvular r in singing. Some versatile artists cleverly alternate between the uvular and the rolled r in their singing (for example, Mlle Lys Gauty).

Your expression, "never or rarely rolls the r's," is in need of correction. One rolls them or does not roll them; there is no middle ground. But when one rolls the r's, one can also make them vibrant; the difference lies here, and I suspect that what you dislike are the vibrant r's. I agree that one must not overdo them.

When you say that Tino Rossi does not roll the r, you are greatly mistaken, for, true Corsican that he is, he *always* rolls them. Dear Monsieur, listen to him carefully (opportunities to do so are not lacking), and you shall be convinced. As for Mme Ninon Vallin's r's, I think they are excellent; for the most part, they are softly rolled and, when necessary, brilliantly vibrant—which is not surprising when you consider that this singer speaks Spanish as if it were her native tongue.

Finally, and this brings us back to the beginning of this article: I do not share your opinion about the students at the Conservatoire, especially those of recent times. I would to heaven that they *could* roll the r's! Presently, we see all too many who cannot do so at all. At any rate, to be perfect, the rolled r must be natural, meaning that it must happen on its own, without effort, while singing. When it is "acquired," to use Mme Louise Matha's expression, the rolled r always makes the listener uncomfortable.

The letter goes on to say:

Obviously, I am incompetent when it comes to vocal technique, but I would very much like to know, if you wouldn't mind telling me, why it is necessary to articulate words differently in singing than in speaking.

I have written at length on this subject in a book entitled *Du Chant,* and I would advise you to read the specific chapter on this subject [Chapter III in the present volume]. I cannot emphasize enough that I am a firm advocate of singing that bears a resemblance to speech. This is the only kind of singing that is truly human; the only kind that stirs emotions, that enraptures. But believe me, the rolled *r* does not stand in the way of such singing.

And yet some music—music that derives its nobility and beauty from lyricism—cannot be adapted to the ordinary inflections of speech by virtue of its character as well as its notation.

I shall always remember the shock I had years ago in Berlin when I went to Lilli Lehmann's home to rehearse *Don Giovanni,* in which she had agreed to sing in Paris under my direction. Wearing a heavy wool sweater and an ungainly hood (it was bitterly cold) under which her beautiful eyes sparkled, she welcomed me with a coarse voice, resting solidly on the low register and speaking with uvular *r*'s of the Prussian variety. I sat down at the piano, and she began to sing. With the first bar, she was transformed:

> *Non sperar se non m'uccidi*
> *Qu'io ti lascia fuggir mai.*

> Do not hope, unless you kill me,
> That I shall ever let you escape.

> (*Don Giovanni,* Act I, Scene 1)

It was a stupendous metamorphosis. Suddenly, her voice became feminine, high, with vibrating resonance. As for the *r*'s, they were rolled, very Italian and bright, surely just as Mozart heard them pronounced and as he himself pronounced them, since he was born in Salzburg.

The Silent E

We are presently witnessing a musical rebirth, a lyrical apotheosis, of the silent *e*. Oh, what an eternal trouble-maker the silent *e* has been for musicians! What a lot of foolishness it has caused! Once it seemed that all the fuss surrounding this question had been put to rest by standard practice and that, whether in serious or light music, we had come to a kind of agreement on that terrible silent *e,* whereby its legitimate claims would be respected, but, at the same time, it would be used with discretion. We had come a long way from the many strained and false accents of the *chansons* performed in cabarets, the thoughtless excesses suggested to a composer like Offenbach by the Italianisms that had invaded French music (as in *Les Brigands:* "*FlamME claiRE*"), and also the carelessness of Debussy in his early period ("*Leurs chasTES amours,*" in the aria from *L'Enfant prodigue*). We had also gotten beyond the complete avoidance of the silent *e* as practiced by certain composers who, intent on realism, could not appreciate the resonance, the tender languor, it adds to verses such as the following:

> *Ariane, ma soeur, de quel amour blessée*
> *Vous mourûtes aux bords où vous fûtes laissée.*
>
> Ariane, my sister, by what wounds of love
> Did you die by the shores where you were forsaken.

If these composers had written music to these verses, they would no doubt have been satisfied with this prosody:

> *Arian', ma soeur, de quel amour blessé*
> *Vous mourût's aux bords . . .*

Fortunately, this erroneous notion did not last long, and those who sanctioned it would have been greatly surprised (or are presently so, since some may still be among us) by the triumphal revenge the silent *e* enjoys today. This resurgence of the *e* is due to the *chanson* and its evolution since the [First World] War. First, it can be traced to the influx and the abuse of foreign *chansons* and to their mediocre translations, the latter often the work of hacks who are illiterate both musically and otherwise. The accents in these translations are continually misplaced: ("*O MA RoSE MariE,*" and so on). It is also due to the number of foreign composers now writing light music, composers who are completely unaware of the unique characteristics of the French language (examples can be found in M. Kurt Weill's *Marie-Galante: "J'attends UN naviRE,"* and so on). More seriously, this revenge of the silent *e* is due to the habits of our own composers who, in order to adjust their prosody to dance rhythms, do not hesitate to distort it, or who, at other times, carelessly and ignorantly scatter silent *e*'s at random. However, more seriously yet, this revenge of the silent *e* has come about due to certain singers of the *chansons* who, for whatever reason (no doubt through lack of taste and general vulgarity), have developed the loathsome habit of emphasizing silent *e*'s by accentuating, prolonging and amplifying them in a ridiculous way. (*"Nous avons cette nuit caché notre tendresSE"*; *"Frémir votre visaGE"*; *"Les nuits de Normandie, si belLES."* *"Le vent du soir qui SE lamente,"* and a perfect example of this abominable style: *"Vous qui passez sans ME voir, Vous dont je guette un REgard."*) Worse yet, they have spread these detestable habits through their many recordings and radio appearances.

The final result of all this is that the singing maidservant or the delivery boy met in the street do the same. Just the other day, on the stairs of the Paris Métro, I heard a very lovely young lady singing: *"Car ton physiQUE est fantastiQUE,"* underlining each of those silent *e*'s, magnifying each one a thousandfold. The effect was unspeakable and reminded me of that fairy-tale princess from whose charming lips frogs emerged.

I must add that silent *e*'s are not the only sounds to be honored so perversely. In general, all short syllables which should be pronounced rapidly or barely touched on receive the same treatment. The repertoire of M. Jean Sablon, among others, superabundantly illustrates this tendency to grant ridiculous emphasis (*"Vous QUI venez dans LA nuit"*), as do his interpretations in general and those of his imitators.

I repeat, it is deplorable that professional singers are not the only victims of this mannerism; it is to be found all around. Nothing is more contagious than bad habits, and the one I have just singled out is painfully evident in singing today, especially in popular music.

There are other bad habits: The whining *portamento,* that "scooping" or "sliding" of the voice which I have frequently denounced and which could never be condemned too strongly. Or the "grace-notes" or "inverted ornaments" (*"pincés renversés,"* as they were called in Rameau's time) which infest so much popular singing today. These embellishments are not written out, but popular singers insert them everywhere for no apparent reason, in everything they sing.

These unjustified ornaments, together with the atrocious scooping of the voice, the exaggerated emphasis on silent *e*'s and on syllables that should be barely audible, result in a style that has nothing to do with what the genuine French *chanson* must be and what it was in former times. Now and then we hear a *chanson* that is well interpreted; but, alas, such occasions are all too rare, and in most cases they put us in the debt of artists who are considered "old hat," "turn-of-the-century" types, or to young singers who wisely seek their inspiration from such mentors. But these rare performances of the true *chanson* only increase the regret and exasperation felt by lovers of singing, forced to witness the sabotage of a light but difficult genre of music in which, at one time, we French excelled.

Articulation

We hear many complaints about singers' poor articulation, and almost always for good reason. This shortcoming has become proverbial, as evidenced by such comments as the answer I received one day from a poet after I had asked him to change a few words in a text I was setting to music: "Why bother? No one understands singers anyway!"

Singers who enunciate clearly are indeed few and far between; I believe this has always been the case. The subject brings to mind an anecdote I heard some years ago: At a musical *soirée,* M. Fauré, after offering a thousand congratulations to Mme de G., who had just sung an aria by Gounod, asked her in feigned ingenuousness: "But, tell me, would you not prefer to sing in French?"

Frequently, it is a preoccupation with the beauty and round-ness of the sound that causes singers to pronounce badly. If words cannot be understood, it is usually due to distorted vowels, though occasionally it is also due to weak consonants, the accentuation of which can, in many cases, modify the "place" and "color" of the sound. Moreover, it is difficult to maintain perfect evenness (*legato*) while at the same time paying attention to the exact mouth position required by the vowels.

In singing, it is not necessary to move the lips grotesquely in order to pronounce well. In my opinion, Ernest Van Dyck, a distinguished artist, was ill-advised to move his mouth in such exaggerated fashion, which merely demonstrated his eagerness to pronounce well.

Maurice Renaud, also an excellent singer, demonstrated a different kind of shortcoming: In his concern with good articulation, he frequently changed the words of the text, asserting that a certain syllable impaired his tone production and that, in such a situation, he was forced to choose between good pronunciation and a bad performance. In addition, this laudable concern for articulation often led him to sing too slowly.

There is much to say about all this; but as I have said a hundred times before, a genuine, thoughtful effort to introduce purity, charm and character into one's pronunciation will result in interesting and lively singing.

But is it always the singer's fault if the listener does not understand the words? Should the blame not sometimes fall to the composer or the conductor? In their effort to obtain a full, colorful and refined orchestration, even some of the best composers forget that they accompany voices and that the larynx cannot compete with a large group of instruments. Their instrumentation is rich, full of clever details, brilliant and fascinating sonorities and charming contrasts. But in all this, what provision has been made for the voice? Not infrequently, a character must sing words crucial to the meaning of the drama or must murmur very softly (expressing tenderness, mystery or even menace), yet suddenly we hear a flute wandering in a range that is too high or too low, a phrase from the violas, a chord from the brasses or a simple stirring of the strings that dominates and obscures the voice, effectively denying the listener the vital clues contained in the text. Elsewhere, in order to be heard, the singer must cut through a deafening hubbub in which three or four themes crisscross one another.

How can one ask the poor soprano in Richard Strauss's *Salomé* to make the words understood? It would be like asking someone to lift the Eiffel Tower off the ground!

And what of composers who write music that is impossible to perform, who ask the sopranos to sing difficult words in the high register, who impose on the tenor several long phrases in his "passage" range?

Conductors, too, cannot escape blame. At theatrical performances (I am not speaking of concerts, in which the singers stand before the orchestra), how often do the conductors really concentrate on bringing out the voices and the words? The moment they are given a complex, "interesting" orchestration, they show very little concern for the poor singers and think only of displaying the instrumental beauties at their disposal.

Wagner has frequently been accused of bringing about the decline of singing because of the strains he imposed on the human voice. This is an unjustified accusation. Wagner's first interpreters were Italian-trained artists used to singing Italian music, a kind of music in which the orchestra had but little significance, where the voice was always in the limelight and could project the most delicate nuances without the slightest fear of being overburdened or even hampered by the orchestral music.

Seeking to give the orchestra an important, often a preponderant role—that of an ongoing commentator—Wagner invented the hidden orchestra. In Bayreuth and Munich, none of the text is lost. The orchestra fulfills its function without ever interfering with the singing, without compelling the singers to "force" in order to be heard. Composers and conductors who do not have the benefit of a hidden orchestra too frequently overlook the place and role of the voices. Unfortunately, however, the general public is often unaware of these matters when attending a performance. The audience fails to hear what the characters are saying and therefore does not understand what is happening onstage. They become bored and ultimately decide not to return.

I was thinking of all this the other evening during a play—no singers, no instrumental interference, just actors whose challenge was to make a text understood. Neither I nor most of the audience could understand several passages. Those actors had no excuse. But, may I say it? Is it fair to blame them when they are so young and inexperienced or perhaps merely docile, complying with the "modern" rules which suggest that anything resembling declamation or good diction is to be despised? I have been witness to the birth of this school, the school of the muttered aside, the important phrase lost in the wings, the school of blurring and glossing over most lines and inflections. Whatever one may say, whatever the slaves of fashion may think, that school is absurd and disastrous. The example of the great actors is an ever-present proof: One can speak correctly and act realistically without stammering. Singer or not, one cannot ignore the laws of articulation and vocal projection. Indeed, when one hears the speech of certain actors, singers appear far less blameworthy, considering all the difficulties they have to overcome.

The Highest Notes

What will become of us? Lily Pons has left France! How will the newspapers fill their columns, which, during her stay with us, glorified her talents day in and day out, enumerated her triumphs, regaled us with the story of her life, overwhelmed us with her opinions, described her many triumphs in America—all this like a theatrical spotlight following the star across the stage.

What marvelous and surprising talents have been discovered during this famous singer's sojourn in Paris! If we were to believe her ardent admirers and a few recent connoisseurs of *bel canto*, she is the only living representative of the French art of singing—even though she has repeatedly declared that she owes everything to her Italian training; even though, except for *Lakmé*, she limits herself, I believe, to the Italian repertory and even though, during this second visit to Paris since the United States enshrined her as the greatest singer of the world, she again sang *Lucia di Lammermoor* at the Opéra (in Italian).

I am quite convinced that Mme Pons has been misquoted in some of her interviews. For example, I can hardly believe that, instead of saying *"les plus grands chefs d'orchestre,"* she said *"les plus grands conducteurs,"*[1] an inappropriate translation of the English word *conductors;* or that, while speaking of Lilli Lehmann (whom she cannot have heard), she is supposed to have declared that that superb artist was "a lyric soprano." (In fact, Mme Lehmann was the archetype of the great dramatic soprano, having at her command all the characteristics of that specific voice type and its particular roles, but also displaying a marvelous agility that allowed her to brilliantly interpret the lighter roles as well.) I doubt that Mme Pons characterized the great Lehmann's range as extending only to high C. (The fact is that in Constanze's first aria in Mozart's *Abduction from the Seraglio,* Mme Lehmann sang some pure, clear and soft D's above high C with the greatest ease and a caressing *pianissimo,* sounding like a faraway flute.)

I was also surprised and dubious at the report that Mme Lily Pons had said it was through hard work that she gained her lovely highest notes—notes that amaze and enchant those who are fond of the vocal stratosphere. Actually, when her teacher, the very remarkable singer Mme Dyna Beumer-Sellier, brought her to me for an audition some ten years ago at Cannes, she already had those notes. It was precisely because of those so easily reached high notes that Mme Maria Gay offered to be the young singer's impresario in America, where anything resembling a sensation is immediately seized upon. Those high notes must have been entirely natural, unless Mme Lily Pons had "worked hard" at them with Mme Beumer-Sellier before our first encounter. But then, what can be said about the Italian training to which Mme Pons has declared herself indebted for the greater part of her vocal artistry? It is well known that over-zealous friends are often clumsy, talking indiscriminately, attributing to the admired one words that were never said and, in general, by their hyperbolic praises, doing more harm than good.

Many people are misinformed about the highest notes of the soprano voice. Having these notes is not, in itself, a proof of superiority but simply a special inherited quality. They are not in the range of the normal soprano voice, which can be perfect and complete without them. Also, their appearance in genuine music is exceptional and is always motivated by the need to give a super-natural aura to a special situation—as, for example, in the arias of the Queen of the Night in Mozart's *Magic Flute.* This role was created by Mme Hofer, Mozart's sister-in-law, who, without effort, could reach the F above high C (which is equivalent to our present E). This singer's natural capability gave the composer the idea of using it to add sparkle to certain passages of the role of this maleficent nocturnal sovereign. For the same purpose, Massenet, in his opera *Esclarmonde*—drawing on the gifts of Sibyl Sander-son, who created the role—ended the sorcerer's invocation to the spirits with the vibrant G above high C.

One should not think that singers possessing the highest of the high notes are extremely rare: Every generation has produced its fair share. Many castratos were capable of reaching those dizzying heights with ease, as well as any number of sopranos who have specialized in such feats and managed to reach ever-higher notes. Only a few years ago, Mlle Galvani galvanized audiences by climbing to a great height in a frenzied, electrifying and prodi-giously rapid fashion. In our day, we have Mlle Erna Sack, whose recordings are available and for whom the A and B-flat above high C are mere child's play. But quite often, those voices possessing a miraculously high register lack fullness in the medium register, in other words, in the expressive register; and it is difficult to name many sopranos (with the exception of Christine Nilsson) who can sing, by turns, "*les soupirs de la sainte et les cris de la fée*" ("the sighs of the saint and the cries of the fairy").

About the "Chest Voice"

About two months ago, I received the following letter from a reader in Rouen. I would have liked to reply promptly, not only because the letter contains some infinitely kind and encouraging words for me as an occasional advocate and defender of the art of singing, but, more particularly, because it deals with a very important vocal problem on which I have for some time eagerly awaited an opportunity to put forward my modest opinion.

Here is the letter—or rather, the relevant portion of the letter:

> I write to ask you for a bit of advice. I never sing chest tones above E, and when it is not necessary to sing loudly, I even perform E-flat and D in a mixed voice. Although I have a solid and full-bodied medium register, it seems to me that in certain cases it is inadequate for loud tones.

Indeed, all depends on circumstances. An expert singer such as you appear to be, Madame, can frequently project enough sound on low notes, *piano,* while using a "mixed voice." But such a singer must also be able to sing these notes as softly as possible with a "chest voice." It is a mistake to think that this poor "chest voice," so discredited today, is reserved for heavy sonorities.

The letter continues:

> I will single out a typical case which has prompted my long letter and on which case I beg your advice. I am referring to Debussy's "Chevaux de bois." For many years, I have sung the following phrase: *"Tournez aux sons du piston vainqueur"* in a mixed voice, *trying not to ruin my voice;* and, sitting at the piano as I sing (since I always play my own accompaniments), the F-sharp on the syllable *"queur"* sounds a little shrill to me, especially in light of the vocal and instrumental *crescendo.*

Obviously. Unless one has an exceptionally solid and full-bodied "passage"[2] (like, for example, Mlle Alice Raveau and the late Conchita Supervia), the F-sharp would never be loud enough in such a case, where, indeed, the word *"vainqueur"* is marked *sff* (*fortissimo*).

I am not sure that Debussy thoroughly understood the mechanics of the human voice; but when he wrote this F-sharp, he undoubtedly "heard" it as strong and vibrant. Thus it is not surprising that, performing it in a medium register, you realized it was too weak. It could not be otherwise. But you did not merely think it was too weak; subconsciously, you also had the impression that it lacked the desired character, *that it did not express what it was meant to express.* Again, you were right, as the following lines of your letter confirm.

> And so, this morning, as I was rehearsing "Les Chevaux de bois," which I was soon to perform for some friends, I was led for the first time, and somehow against my will, to support those last notes with a full chest voice. At first, I startled, because the effect is somewhat vulgar; but after repeating it a couple of times, I realized it was not offensive, since the general mood of Verlaine's poem is one of loud popular rejoicing, exactly as Debussy has conceived it.

Here, Madame, you are perfectly right. By uttering that F-sharp in a "chest voice," you produced a full tone, clearly audible, facilitating good projection of the word. Moreover, you satisfied the obvious intention of the composer by evoking through a slightly vulgar tone color the picturesque vision of a country fair. But you had to be naturally able to do it, you had to possess that special sonority, your palette of sounds had to include that particular color—in short, you had to be able to produce that F-sharp with a "chest voice."

You will notice, Madame, that I always place the words "chest voice" between quotation marks; the fact is that the expression is as inaccurate as "palatal voice," "head voice," and so on. Such expressions are, according to a voice expert, only conventional words that facilitate ready understanding, for the voice is not produced in the chest any more than it is produced at the palate or in the head. By saying "chest tones," "head tones," and so on, we merely designate the area where these tones resonate more or less exclusively. This said, I will drop the quotation marks in the interests of simplicity and say that the current denigration of the chest voice is absurd—this low opinion would have made all the great singers of the past shrug their shoulders impatiently, for these tones are essential to the beauty of the voice.

One has only to read the accounts of master teachers, to recall the leading singers we have heard and their own comments on this subject, or to listen to recordings made by the great *cantatrices* to be convinced that, first, chest tones are absolutely necessary to obtain richness, power, warmth, in any female voice; and, second, the use of chest tones has never caused harm to the upper register of the voice, as some would have us believe.

To prove this, I shall limit myself to two or three telling examples. Lilli Lehmann, who, up to the last years of her life, performed with incomparable brilliance and purity the difficult high passages in *The Abduction from the Seraglio,* always ended the phrase *"des Himmels Segen belohne dich"* with a full chest-voice G in the medium register, even after the trill on the preceding A. And, although she ranged from indescribable sweetness to bravura high notes in the Act II aria "Non mi dir" from *Don Giovanni,* she did not hesitate—in Act I, when Donna Anna cries out for help—to scream (this is the right word): *"Gente, servi!"* on the A, middle range, chest voice. This is of course an exceptional case; nevertheless, it shows that this famous artist, despite the frequent use of chest tones (even some dangerous ones), left her marvelous top register intact.

Mme Emma Calvé recorded during a single session the aria of Mysoli with its hushed tones, the card scene from *Carmen* and the "Marseillaise," using chest tones that take your breath away. Melba's recordings of 1906, particularly the one including the "Air de la Folie" from the Thomas opera *Hamlet,* are irrefutable proof of the compatibility of a strongly supported chest voice and a brilliant, clear and agile high register.

To repeat, Madame: All the great singers have used the chest voice in the low register; they have done so, to be sure, with discernment and taste, with force or with tenderness as expression required. By low register I mean, for the contralto, the one that begins at E below middle C, and for the soprano, the one that extends from middle C up to F, first space. I consider these notes the pivotal points at which the voice must turn; it should be possible to produce them in either the chest or the medium register. Many artists will go higher in chest tones if necessary. But this is not advisable, though Manuel Garcia, brother of the great Malibran and of Pauline Viardot, says that, in women's voices, the chest register may extend up to C-sharp or D (I shall comment later on this matter). What is sure, for Saint-Saëns told me this, is that when Duprez was teaching Mlle Miolan (later Mme Carvalho, who sang the premieres of Juliette, Baucis and Mireille in Gounod's operas,[3] all particularly high roles), he had her sing runs up to B-flat in chest tones. "And," added Saint-Saëns, "she must have had a very sturdy voice!"

I agree; but there is a world of difference between this approach and banning chest tones in a register where they are natural and normal and serve an artistic purpose. Nothing is weaker, more woeful, duller and more distressing than the mixed register used below F. Many teachers today say that if the mixed voice is "correctly placed," "correctly set" and sounds good in the forehead cavities, it can replace the chest voice. Never, never, Madame, can this be a true substitute. After hearing so many thin-voiced Marguerites (though their voices were not thin because their chests lacked breadth, alas!), I remember the pleasure I had at the two thousandth performance of *Faust,* hearing Mlle Yvonne Gall articulate on a well-supported, distinctive timbre, those famous words, inaudible for the past few years: *"Je voudrais bien savoir quel était ce jeune homme"* ("I would very much like to know who that young man was").

Following the death of M. Maton, who had been her regular accompanist, I often had the great honor of accompanying Mme Patti. By this time, she avoided the high altitudes even though she still had an admirable A, a beautiful B-flat and even a C that she reached valiantly and quickly. But the medium range of her voice was still incredibly velvety, limpid, subtle and generous. Considering the volume and caliber of her voice, she could have reached the low notes without having recourse to the chest voice, unlike so many female singers of our time who, already out of breath when singing A and G, must descend to those depths via the chest voice. All the same, in Zerlina's first aria from *Don Giovanni* and in Cherubino's second aria from *The Marriage of Figaro,* Mme Patti used a well-supported and extremely mellow chest voice in all the low registers, to the delight of the listening ear and to Mozart's greater glory.

The female singers I have mentioned so far, those who do not hesitate—without thinking about it—to use the chest voice in the low register, are all sopranos singing particularly high roles. In the same category, I might add Mme Nordica, Mme Gianina Russ, Mme Kousnetzoff, Mme Ponselle, Mme Blanche Marchesi (who, at the age of seventy-five, has just made some remarkable recordings), Mme Emma Eames, Mme Alda, Mme Geraldine Farrar (who, in the third act of *Manon,* sang some poignant chest notes), Mme Marguerite Carré, Mlle Garden, Mme Fanny Heldy, Mme Ninon Vallin, Mme Norena, and so forth and so on. It would be appropriate to add to this long list some particularly high sopranos, some illustrious specialists in light vocalises (*coloraturas* as they are rather ridiculously described today in view of the fact that the word *vocalise* is *Koloratur* in German)—veritable birds, in short, such as Mmes Barrientos, Verlet, Landouzy, Hidalgo, Tetrazzini and Marcella Sembrich. To this count, I must add the soprano Erna Sack, who to the best of my knowledge possesses the highest notes of any living singer, but who nonetheless, upon leaving the highest vocal ranges where she performs with such ease, fearlessly returns

Lily Pons, French soprano (1904–1976), in the title role of Donizetti's *Lucia di Lammermoor*. Photo by De Bellis. Courtesy Andrew Farkas.

to the medium range by means of a few strongly emphasized notes and with no recourse to the mixed voice.

I repeat: Not one of these artists—and we have their recordings to confirm my observations—not one has been reluctant to use the chest voice, and this is as it should be. Furthermore, Fauré believes that the E (bottom line of the staff) should be sung by the soprano in the mixed voice only in the exceptional case. To this I would add that a soprano should use the chest voice above the F only on the rarest occasions.

However, as M. Max d'Ollone[4] once told me in a letter, "there is a misunderstanding. Often, one thinks one is hearing chest notes when they are actually guttural, harsh, unpleasant sounds that are harmful to the voice." This misunderstanding, which is spreading from day to day, has been with us for a long time. Marietta Alboni, that incomparable interpreter of Lucrezia Borgia, with the lowest contralto voice of all the contraltos, became indignant, we are told, when someone praising her low notes called them "chest" notes. The imposing lady was not amused!

And M. d'Ollone adds: "As you say, the true chest tone can be very soft. One must be able to sustain it evenly."

Evidently. If that F which is so important to me can be sung in either the chest voice or the mixed voice (which would result in an evenly sustained tone), then the troublesome problem of the rough transition, the *distacco,* disappears. So much the better; and yet, how could we not agree with Fauré's opinion that "the rough passage from the chest to the head voice has a most unpleasant effect; however, who could deny that, among a few exceptional singers, there is something particularly sympathetic and touching about this *distacco?*"

Let us go back to M. d'Ollone's letter. "All Italian *chanteuses* use the chest tone. In Italy, people would hiss in disapproval if one sang Amneris or Dalila with the low register in head tones." Well said. However, for some years now, many voice teachers have forbidden the use of the chest voice even among contraltos. If their views were to prevail, contraltos would disappear altogether. In fact, they are already scarce; to be convinced of this fact, one has only to attend performances of *Samson et Dalila, Hamlet, La Favorita* or other works calling for a contralto. The contralto will eventually become extinct, like animal or plant species we fail to protect; so future generations will be able to learn how a real contralto sounded only by listening to the recordings of Mmes Deschamps-Jéhin, Maria Gay, Kirby-Lunn, Schumann-Heink and the amazing Clara Butt.

"No doubt," continues M. d'Ollone, "there are female singers who do not naturally possess chest tones and who, wishing to support low notes either for a dramatic purpose or in order to avoid being 'swallowed' by the orchestra, resort to unpleasant guttural sounds."

To this very accurate observation there can be no better answer than the following paragraph by Fauré:

> The most effective way to help sopranos in finding this register, when they need it, is imitation. No physiological definition will help them. Sopranos will most rapidly acquire it by trying to imitate the voices of young boys, the voices heard in children's choirs or the voices of contraltos.

Fauré's mention of contraltos and the voices of young boys in the same breath confirms, with all due deference to Alboni, that the contralto actually does use chest tones. Théophile Gautier saw and heard clearly when he compared that particular voice with the ancient sculpture of an ambiguous, outstretched form so discreetly exhibited in our museums:

> *Rêve de poète et d'artiste,*
> *Tu m'as bien des nuits occupé,*
> *Et mon caprice qui persiste*
> *Ne convient pas qu'il s'est trompé.*

Mais seulement il se transpose.
Et, passant de la forme au son,
Trouve dans sa métamorphose
La jeune fille et le garçon.

Que tu me plais, ô timbre étrange,
Son double, homme et femme à la fois,
Contralto, bizarre mélange,
Hermaphrodite de la voix!

Dream of the poet and the artist,
You have haunted me for many nights,
And my persistent fantasy
Will not admit it has erred.

But then it is transformed.
And, passing from form to sound,
Finds in its metamorphosis
The young lass as well as the lad.

How you please me, oh strange timbre,
Twofold sound, man and woman at once,
Contralto, bizarre mixture,
Hermaphrodite of the voice!

Reading these verses (the whole poem is admirable) and reflecting upon their contents, one is tempted to conclude, as M. d'Ollone believes, that "this phobia of chest tones" may have obscure psychological origins—that some women feel "a subconscious modesty, a scruple that is more moral than esthetic, when singing sounds that are too virile." This is very possible; his reflections on matters of singing are extremely thoughtful and proceed from a keen intellect. One only wishes that M. d'Ollone would explore these matters in greater depth.

Meanwhile, it is most important to eliminate that unfortunate prejudice which deprives the art of singing of one of its most beautiful means of expression. "One cannot ignore," writes Fauré, "the profound effects that women create by using their chest register." It is truly presumptuous to pretend to a deeper knowledge than such a master, to deny the truth of his observations or the accounts of great artists, great connoisseurs who have excelled in the art of singing, who have penetrated the mysteries of this art at the height of its perfection and magnificence. It is equally presumptuous to disregard the examples of the many excellent female singers who have depended upon this approach that is absurdly condemned and prohibited today.

After these extensive explanations which, despite their length, explore only incompletely the important question of the female chest voice, I must return to the letter that began this discussion to quote another phrase from my knowledgeable reader in Rouen.

Still on the matter of the F-sharp that she projects with a full chest voice in Debussy's "Les Chevaux de bois," she writes:

> You may be sure that I will not make a habit of this particular type of tone production, for I have no desire whatsoever to imitate those "realistic" singers who are presently so highly regarded but whom I do not especially admire.

I have substituted the word *realistic* for that used in the letter, as the latter could be construed more negatively than my correspondent intended. Here she is referring to music-hall artists. Formerly these artists were few indeed, but now they are innumerable; and because of poor practices due to several causes, or because of special training, they use the chest voice exclusively or almost exclusively. That unvarying tone production gives their singing, especially in the medium range, a roughness of tone and feeling particularly suitable to expressing rude sentiments and moods of great excitement (violent sensual love, savage hatred, loud or crude gaiety, bellicose patriotism and so on) and which, even if devoid of art, can occasionally result in beautiful effects. But this tone production, used with discernment, taste, and in the right degree—as some *chanteuses* I have had the opportunity to observe and admire have ably demonstrated—can give the music especially rich coloration, a mellowness and intensity that the mixed voice is often incapable of achieving. And so, even though I have reservations about this approach to singing, I cannot deny that in certain cases it holds a powerful appeal.

Thérésa was the first *chanteuse* I heard singing in this style. This famous *diseuse* [a female *diseur,* a crooner or pop-singer] sang simple country songs in her youth, using a normal voice. Following a severe attack of laryngitis, her vocal range changed completely. Her register, lowered by an octave, sounded like that of a tenor-baritone, and her low notes were fuller and richer than those of a tenor. Naturally, this change forced her to change her repertoire: A new Thérésa emerged, majestic and moving. Her success and her talent led to widespread imitation. Some far more sophisticated artists, whose particular vocal qualities prompted them to imitate Thérésa, perhaps unconsciously adopted her technique when performing works of a higher level and a style inaccessible to this essentially popular singer.

I still remember the way Mme Edouard Lalo, a remarkable musician and expert singer, used to emphasize and draw out certain classical excerpts and *mélodies* composed by her illustrious husband, such as the *mélodie* "L'Esclave": One had the impression of hearing a superb cello. I also remember a woman named Mme Collier who enjoyed a well-deserved vogue in exclusive musical circles for several years. She had the appearance of a jovial, middleclass housewife; yet when she sang, she sounded like a bacchante or an Amazon. Her interpretation of "Les Gars d'Irlande" by Augusta Holmès was positively spine-tingling.

In her younger years, Augusta Holmès herself had an ample soprano voice with an impressive range. Later, her voice changed greatly, and she was transformed into another Thérésa. Following this change, she interpreted her own works in that singular fashion the poet Gautier described: in the "twofold, hermaphroditic voice" that suggests both man and woman.

Taken to be the epitome of grace, daring, and charming gaiety, this fashion of singing "à la Thérésa" was incomparably represented by Mlle Jeanne Gouzien (today, Mme Pierre Jeanniot). What exquisite style, what graceful diction she brought to her interpretations of the works of Offenbach, of French or Spanish songs, singing in her teenager's voice, merry at one moment and melancholy the next; what refined sentiment she poured into her performances of the duets of Schumann, Mendelssohn or Saint-Saëns in which I joined her in the company of Alphonse Daudet and his entourage, all under the spell of her gifts and youthful talent.

But of all the *cantatrices* for whom the chest voice was natural and usual and who ventured only occasionally into other registers, and then only with extreme caution, as one might enter a danger zone—the most astonishing I have known was Mme Jean de Reszke, née Marie de Goulaine. Everything about her was beautiful, refined, sweet, fascinating: her charming face, her bright and somber glance, her ravishing and sad smile, the way she held her head and moved—in every way, she was without equal. As for her voice, I never heard anything like it before and I doubt whether anyone will again. It is impossible for me to describe it, for I have never succeeded in analyzing it. The voice itself was imbued with mystery, as was the singing it enveloped in its spell. It was a magic emanation, an intoxicating essence. Its sound was ethereal and golden at the same time; moreover, this voice was endowed with an amazing agility that made the most rapid excerpts from the Italian repertoire a simple matter. I particularly recall an evening when Mme de Reszke and the Countess of Guerne, sitting side by side in armchairs after dinner, sang a duet from *Semiramide*. They had not rehearsed, and they made a game of this Rossini repertoire which was so familiar to them both.

But this was not the music Mme de Reszke preferred to sing. Her great love was the music of Schubert and Schumann and particularly that of Gounod, which she had sung since childhood and, so to speak, in the lap of the master. Of the *mélodie* "Au Rossignol," she created a deep and boundless nocturne, resounding with infinite echos; and when she sang the short aria of the shepherd in *Sapho,* one felt one was actually "seeing the golden Cyclades emerge from the azure."

Furthermore, her memory was inexhaustible; she knew everything by heart, and she could, on the spur of the moment, sing anything from *Tristan,* the *Mastersingers* and the *Ring,* from any Viennese operetta (in the original language, of course, for she knew and spoke several languages with perfection) or from the French Romantic repertoire ranging from Méhul to Massenet. One would need several pages to describe the exact nature of Mme de Reszke's wholly spontaneous art—she had never taken lessons, properly speaking; God was her only teacher. I limit myself to this appraisal by Jean de Reszke himself: "Marie is the greatest *chanteuse* I have ever met."

As I noted earlier, Thérésa's second incarnation gave rise to a throng of imitators. There was a period of quiet, but now they are springing up again. Today false Thérésas are multiplying as if being mass-produced. It goes without saying that they have adapted to current tastes and the popular rhythms that surround us and largely dominate the singing circuits and recording studios—"*J'l'ai dans la peau, mon beau gosse, . . .*" ("He's under my skin, my beautiful kid, . . ."). Everyone is at it. Lyricists and composers vie with each other in the pursuit of bestiality and mindless banality. Meanwhile, the chest voice forced upwards has become the key to success. I know several women who are able to sing quite normally but who insist upon joining the already inflated ranks of the false Thérésas. Some who perform in this style may have desirable qualities, charm and even talent. But aside from these few singers of merit, others we could name degrade the vocal art by their sentimental gushing and amorous belchings! These gross sensualists lead one to detest the chest voice, which is surely one very good reason among many to wage war upon them.

Can you believe it? I have still more to say about the chest voice. Is it my fault if I have received and continue to receive so many letters on this subject which some, no doubt, find rather dull, but which is of the greatest importance for those who are interested in vocal art and saddened by its decline? Many of these letters should be quoted and discussed in detail, but I do not wish to try my readers' patience.

Still, I cannot resist the temptation of noting that, among the people who have written to me, those who agree with my ideas are quite often experienced artists who have had successful careers, which goes far to prove the case that the use of chest tones is not as disastrous as many have claimed with inexplicable tenacity in the last few years. "You are a hundred times right," Mme Emma Calvé wrote, adding: "I am convinced that I have preserved my voice thanks to well-supported low notes which I consider the foundation of the vocal apparatus." The well-known singer Mme Edouard Colonne reminded me of the special effects she was able to obtain (in fact, these effects are still vivid in my memory) by using chest tones in her interpretation of the "Griffes d'or"; she mentioned other instances as well when she used that particularly rich register of her flexible and expressive voice.

On the other hand, a woman from London whose name I shall not disclose wrote a somewhat confused letter in which she vehemently declared herself a staunch enemy of chest tones. She told me that she had possessed a very beautiful voice, originally thought to be contralto and then mezzo-soprano, until the baritone Alban Grand (who, under the name of Albany, had some success in the provinces and in London during and after the war) discovered she was really a dramatic soprano. All this is quite remote from our present topic, but she goes on to say: "Alban Grand should have been the premier baritone in France! Moreover, like Battistini, he never used chest tones."

Just a minute; this is getting interesting. I wish to remind my correspondent that I had spoken exclusively of female voices since, before reading her letter, I was unaware that a man could possibly sing in the low or medium register in any manner other than through the use of chest tones. But what left me totally dumbfounded was this statement about the famous bass Pol Plançon, which my lively opponent advanced as her ultimate and irrefutable argument: "Plançon always used chest notes, and *Plançon died of consumption!*" This devastating observation may, in my opinion, shed a new light on the origin of pulmonary tuberculosis, so I will humbly refer it to the esteemed professor of medicine Fernand Bezançon for his consideration . . .

Respect for the Text

Last Thursday, an extraordinary event occurred at the Opéra-Comique. The musicians in the orchestra pit and the conductor himself were left with mouth agape, as were the members of the audience who were familiar with the score of *Lakmé*. I believe that the gentlemen from the controller's office, the inspectors, ushers, stagehands, electricians and even the kind concierge, M. Léopold, who must have heard the news immediately, were also dumbfounded, stupefied, petrified, not knowing whether to approve, protest, rejoice or be shocked. In short, it was an event of major importance in the history of theater, an event so unforeseen and so unforeseeable that only the audacity of a great and unsophisticated artist could have brought it about.

Here it is. M. André Pernet was singing the role of Nilakantha. During the aria "Lakmé, ton doux regard se voile," this singer made a momentous decision that stunned everyone: When he came to the phrase, "*Mais je veux retrouver ton sourire*" ("But I want to find your smile again"), he sang *what Delibes had written!* In other words, he simply sang the printed triplet in strict time, without holding the second note, without observing that absurd *fermata* which has slowly but surely become a habit with singers and with the public and has thus become one of those "traditions" that no one has the courage to oppose. Traditions of this kind spread, they take root, and with countless other such traditions, they result in the misinterpretation and distortion of all the works in the repertoire, one after the other. Sung as M. Pernet sang it, that phrase is again expressive and moving, while that unlikely, unforgivable and ridiculous "*re-----trouver*" had destroyed all emotion. Instead of listening to a performer who merely pronounced words, we heard a singer who sang notes as written.

If only M. Pernet's accomplishment might serve as an example and chart a new course. After all, in early times, statuary was born in a single stroke when the first primitive sculptor dared to cut an arm away from the body where it had always been tightly welded! If Nilakantha's simple triplet, performed at a normal tempo as the composer required, could become the starting point of an era of good taste and truth in theatrical singing, M. Pernet would have rendered an immense service to his profession and earned an additional right to the gratitude of all musicians.

Traditions

How many errors and stupidities have been perpetrated in the name of those silly traditions which grow up on established music like poisonous mushrooms! If, someday, one could hear a work from the standard repertoire free of these wretched parasites, one would have a feeling of freshness, a sense of witnessing a revival.

Then a Manon might sing without affectation: "*Je suis encore tout étourdie*" ("I am still quite dizzy"), with only a very slight *ritenuto*, but not "*tout étourdi-----e*" to flaunt her lovely and soft G. Instead of holding the syllable "*Par*" for a full second (a second is too long!) then spluttering incomprehensibly: "*donnezamonbavardage*" and ending (as Massenet imprudently tolerated in the second edition) with, "*J'en suis à mon premier* (stop and breathe) *voyage,*" she would go on at a rapid but even and reasonable tempo with these very ordinary words: "*Pardonnez à mon bavardage, j'en suis à mon premier voyage*" ("Pardon my chattering, this is my first trip"). Thus she would end the musical phrase as written in the first edition, the one that good taste suggests as being the most sincere. Such a Manon would not transform the adieux to her "*petite table*" into an unending and heart-rending lament; in the "Cours la Reine" act, she would not suddenly become asthmatic to a degree that prevents her from exclaiming: "*Suis-je gentille ainsi?*" ("Am I pleasing like this?") without having to stop and breathe between "*gentille*" and "*ainsi.*" During the duet in the seminary, she would render the phrase "*N'est-ce plus ma voix?*" ("Is it no longer my voice?") in a charming and beguiling way (which would mean: "Is this not the voice that once seduced, calmed, caressed you?") rather than ending it in an agile and rapid sort of pirouette (which means instead: "Is this no longer my pop-singer's voice?") Such a Manon, even if she is not ravishing, even if she does not have a stupendous voice, would far better satisfy Massenet's wishes, and those of the Abbé Prévost, than all those luscious and ridiculously egocentric Manons who have invaded our opera houses.

And yet, is it not Massenet's own fault if so many unfortunate errors are constantly made in the interpretation of his delightful masterpiece? Indeed, as I have already said, the second edition has nuances and tempo markings that are not consistent with the first one. He made those changes after the new production of his opera at the Opéra-Comique in 1891 with Sibyl Sanderson. That brilliant artist was a spoiled child; with a smile, she asked for and obtained with little difficulty some modifications that the master understandably granted, since talent and prestige have their privileges. But he was unwise to extend these exceptional privileges to everyone by replacing the old indications in the score with new ones.

What I have said about the role of Manon could also be said about that of Des Grieux (among the roles that have suffered most from those persistent "traditions"), as well as the role of Lescaut, which has been been subjected to every sort of distortion in the name of defiance, and, finally, about the role of the Count. I have heard recent interpretations of this role that were marked by harshness and shouting—painful for someone who remembers the calm and dignity that Fugère, for example, brought to this character.

Faust, Roméo, Mireille, Carmen—all these and others beg for corrections of a similar kind. It is high time to reverse the present state of affairs, which I am not the only one to deplore, as it has been repeatedly lamented. A completely new look at the repertoire is imperative. Putting things back in order will require an untiring zeal and patience from conductors and coaches, and a clear sense of their responsibilities from singers themselves. One cannot remind these performers too often that their task is to serve music, not to adapt it to their caprices; that the more closely and carefully they serve it, the greater will be their chance of success—at least, the type of success sought by true artists; and, finally, the clenching argument in our time, that such success can, on occasion, be every bit as profitable as a more gaudy and glittering career.

These excerpts from the chapter "Remarques sur le chant" first appeared in Reynaldo Hahn's *Thèmes variés* (Paris, 1946).

[1] [The French "*conducteur*" refers primarily to the driver of an automobile or conductor on a train.]

[2] [The "passage" or "*passaggio*" usually occurs at the E-flat, E-natural, F-natural

and F-sharp just above middle C.]

³ [Three operas by Charles Gounod: *Roméo et Juliette* (1867), *Philémon et Baucis* (1860) and *Mireille* (1864).]

⁴ [Max d'Ollone (1875–1959), French composer who studied with Massenet.]

Emma Calvé, French soprano (1858–1942). Photo by Aimé Dupont. Courtesy Andrew Farkas.

The Recorded Legacy of
Reynaldo Hahn

by William R. Moran

Reynaldo Hahn left recordings as a singer (baritone), and often as an accompanist for his own singing [I]; as an accompanist for other singers [II]; as conductor [III]; and as a speaker [IV]. All recordings were made in Paris, those from 1909 through 1919 by the acoustical process; all others were electrical. The recordings are listed in each category in chronological order. Each is assigned a discography number. An asterisk indicates that an explanatory note will be found in the note section at the end. The first number in the second line of each listing is the matrix number assigned at the time of recording by the manufacturer; this is followed by the date of recording. Numbers following the date are the catalog numbers under which the disc was released. The absence of any catalog numbers indicates that the recording was unpublished. Letters in brackets at extreme right indicate reissues on long-playing recordings which are detailed at the end. ("rr" indicates a dubbing.)

I. RECORDINGS AS SINGER

Compagnie Française du Gramophone

All with piano; thought to be self-accompanied. In French unless otherwise noted. (u = 10″; v = 12″; Black Label where issued.)

1.	Offrande (Verlaine; Hahn)	14561u	8 Apr. '09	—	—	—
2.	Mélodie (no further information)	14562u	8 Apr. '09	—	—	—
3.	Mélodie (no further information)	14563u	8 Apr. '09	—	—	—
4.	L'île heureuse (Mikhaël; Chabrier)	14967u	9 Jul. '09	—	—	—
5.	Maid of Athens (Vierge d'Athénes) (Byron; Gounod) (in English)	14968u	9 Jul. '09	—	—	—
6.	Chanson du mai (Gounod)	14969u	9 Jul. '09	4-43073	P-116	[A;B]
7.	Le Cimetière de campagne (Vicaire; Hahn)	14970u	9 Jul. '09	4-32074	P-117	[B]
8.	AMADIS DE GAULE: Bois épais (Jean-Baptiste Lully)	14971u	9 Jul. '09	—	—	—
9.	L'île heureuse (Mikhaël; Chabrier)	14986u	21 Aug. '09	4-32075	P-117	[B]
10.	AMADIS DE GAULE: Bois épais (Jean-Baptiste Lully)	14987u	21 Aug. '09	—	—	—
11.	Maid of Athens (Vierge d'Athénes) (Byron; Gounod) (in English)	14988u	21 Aug. '09	—	—	—
12.	La Tour Saint-Jacques (Darcier)	14989u	21 Aug. '09	4-32076	P-116	—

No.	Title	Matrix	Date	Issue	IRCC	P	Notes
13.	Offrande (Verlaine; Hahn)	14900u	21 Aug. '09	4-32077	IRCC 3053rr	----	----
14.	Musette du 17ième siècle (Anon.)	14993u	24 Aug. '09	----	----	----	----
15.	Chanson du printemps (Tourneux; Gounod)	14994u	24 Aug. '09	----	----	----	----
16.	(Les) PÊCHEURS DE PERLES: De mon amie (Bizet)	14995u	24 Aug. '09	----	----	----	[B]
17.	(Les) PÊCHEURS DE PERLES: De mon amie (Bizet)	14995½u	24 Aug. '09	4-32078	IRCC 3053rr	----	[B]
18.	Musette du 17ième siècle (Anon.)	15454u	22 Nov. '09	4-32013	----	P-104	----
19.	AMADIS DE GAULE: Bois épais (Jean-Baptiste Lully)	15455u	22 Nov. '09	----	----	----	----
20.	La barcheta (Herra; Hahn)	15456u	22 Nov. '09	4-32014	----	P-104	[A;B]
21.*	Le Lever (no further information)	15457u	22 Nov. '09	----	----	----	----
22.*	Le Lever (no further information)	15457½u	22 Nov. '09	----	----	----	----
23.	AMADIS DE GAULE: Bois épais (Jean-Baptiste Lully)	16246u	18 Jan. '11	4-32240	----	P-170	[C]
24.	Chanson du printemps (Tourneux; Gounod)	16247u	18 Jan. '11	----	----	----	----
25.	Chanson du printemps (Tourneux; Gounod)	16434u	22 Apr. '11	----	----	----	----
26.	(Le) DEVIN DU VILLAGE: L'amour selon sa fantaisie (Jean-Jacques Rousseau)	16435u	22 Apr. '11	4-32239	----	P-170	----

No.	Title	Matrix	Date	Take	P-no.	
27.	(Le) DEVIN DU VILLAGE: L'amour selon sa fantaisie (Jean-Jacques Rousseau)	16435½u	22 Apr. '11	------	---	---
28.	Venezia: Ché pecà? (F. dall'Ongaro; Hahn)	20838u	27 Oct. '19	4-32406	P-371	[A]
29.	Les Cigales (Rosemonde Gérard; Chabrier)	20839u	27 Oct. '19	4-32468	P-405	---
30.	Offrande (Verlaine; Hahn)	20840u	27 Oct. '19	4-32405	P-371	[B]
31.	La Paix (de Banville; Hahn)	20841u	27 Oct. '19	4-32469	P-404	[B]
32.	Biondina bella (fr. song cycle "Biondina": Zaffira; Gounod) (in Italian)	03234v	27 Oct. '19	------	---	---
33.	Toutes les fleurs (Rostand; Chabrier)	03235v	27 Oct. '19	------	---	---
34.	Au rossignol (Lamartine; Gounod)	03236v	27 Oct. '19	------	---	---
35.	MAÎTRE WOLFRAM: Les larmes (F. J. Méry; Ernest Reyer)	20861u	4 Nov. '19	4-32470	P-404	[B]
36.	COSÌ FAN TUTTI: Un'aura amorosa (Mozart)	20862u	4 Nov. '19	------	---	---
37.	Chanson du juillet (no further information)	20863u	4 Nov. '19	------	---	---
38.	COSÌ FAN TUTTI: Un'aura amorosa (Mozart)	20864u	4 Nov. '19	------	---	---
39.	Chanson du printemps (Tourneux; Gounod)	20865u	4 Nov. '19	4-32467	P-405	---
40.	L'Enamourée (de Banville; Hahn)	03248v	4 Nov. '19	------	---	---

No.	Title	Matrix	Date				
41.	COSÌ FAN TUTTI: Un'aura amorosa (Mozart) (in Italian)	20948u	2 Dec. '19	4-32561	----	P-471	[A;B]
42.	Biondina bella (fr. song cycle "Biondina": Zaffira; Gounod) (in Italian)	03292v	2 Dec. '19	----	----	----	----
43.	L'Enamourée (de Banville; Hahn)	03293v	2 Dec. '19	032429	----	W-524	[A;B]
44.	Au rossignol (Lamartine; Gounod)	03294v	2 Dec. '19	----	----	----	----
45.	Toutes les fleurs (Rostand; Chabrier)	03295v	2 Dec. '19	032398	----	W-434	----
46.	Biondina bella (fr. song cycle "Biondina": Zaffira; Gounod) (in Italian)	03296v	2 Dec. '19	032397	----	W-434	----

Disques "Columbia"

All with piano by Hahn unless otherwise noted.
All 10" except No. 47. In French unless otherwise noted.
(All dates are estimated from matrix numbers and release dates.)

No.	Title	Matrix	Date				
47.*	Maid of Athens (Vierge d'Athénes) (Byron; Gounod) (in English)	LX 374	1928	----	----	HMB 14	[A;B]
48.	Aimons-nous (Barbier; Gounod)	L 393	1928	D 2020	----	----	[A;B]
49.	L'île heureuse (Mikhaël; Chabrier)	L 394	1928	----	----	----	----
50.	Chanson d'avril (Bouilhet; Bizet, Op. 21, No. 1)	L 563	1929	D 2021	----	----	[A]
51.	L'île heureuse (Mikhaël; Chabrier)	L 564	1929	D 2020	----	----	[A]

No.	Title	L	Year	D		[Code]
52.	LA BOULANGÈRE A DES ÉCUS: a) Les Charbonniers et fariniers (Offenbach) b) Un homme d'un vrai mérite . . . Que voulez-vous	L 579	1929	D 2022	3756-X	[A;B]
53.	(Les) PÊCHEURS DE PERLES: Ô Nadir doit expirer (Bizet)	L 580	1929	D 2021	----	[A]
54.	(Le) DEVIN DU VILLAGE: L'amour selon sa fantaisie (Jean-Jacques Rousseau)	L 581	1929	D 2022	----	[B]
55.	Si tu veux, Mignonne (G. Boyer; Massenet) (pf. J. Benvenuti)	L 1070	1930	D 2029	----	[A;B]
56.	L'Absent (V. Hugo; Gabriel Fauré) (pf. J. Benvenuti)	L 1071	1930	----	----	----
57.	Le Plus Beau Présent (Magre; Hahn) (pf. J. Benvenuti?)	L 1072	1930	----	----	----
58.	J'ai passé par là (Répertoire de Thérésa) (pf. J. Benvenuti?)	L 1073	1930	----	----	----
59.	CIBOULETTE: C'est sa banlieue (Hahn) (pf. J. Benvenuti?)	L 1089	1930	----	----	----
60.*	(Le) Parfum impérissable (L. de Lisle; G. Fauré, Op. 76, No. 1) (pf. J. Benvenuti)	L 1090	1930	D 2029	----	[A;B]
61.	L'Absent (V. Hugo; Gabriel Fauré)	L 2399	1932	----	----	----
62.	Le Retour du marin (Chanson populaire poitevine) (Har. Julien Tiersot)	L 2400	1932	BF 1	----	[A;B]
63.	Le Pauvre Laboureur (Chanson populaire bressanne) (Har. Julien Tiersot)	L 2401	1932	BF 1	----	[A;B]
64.	La Tour Saint-Jacques (Darcier)	L 2402	1932	----	----	----

II. RECORDINGS AS ACCOMPANIST TO OTHER SINGERS

Arthur Endrèze (baritone): (Pathé-Marconi)

65. Psyché—Je suis jaloux (Corneille; Paladilhe)   PG 88
    CFT 3137   1936?

66. Études latines No. 10: Phyllis (L. de Lisle; R. Hahn)
    CFT 3138   1936?   PG 88

Guy Ferrant (tenor): (French Columbia)

67. (Le) TEMPS D'AIMER: Lettre d'amour (Hahn)
    CL 6162   1934?   DF 2156

68. (Le) TEMPS D'AIMER: Le chien fidèle (Hahn)
    CL 6163   1934?   DF 2156

69. Chansons grises No. 6: Paysage triste (Verlaine; Hahn)
    CL 6456   1936   DF 2305

70. (Le) Plus Beau Présent (Magre; Hahn)
    CL 6462   1936?   DF 2305

71. Je me metz en vostre mercy (Charles d'Orléans; Hahn)
    CL ?   1937?   DF 2435

72. (La) CARMÉLITE: Sommes-nous pas trop heureux? (Hahn)
    CL ?   1937?   DF 2435

Ninon Vallin (soprano): (Odéon)

73. Infidélité (Gautier; Hahn)
    ki 3477   1930?   188738   195088   [D]

74. D'une prison (Verlaine; Hahn)
    ki 3478-2   1930?   188738   RO 20120   20505   [D;E]

75.	Le Printemps (de Banville; Hahn) ki 3479 1930?	188739	190598	20506		[D;E]
76.	L'Air (de Banville; Hahn) ki 3480-2 1930?	188739	RO 20120	20506		[D;E]
77.	Les Étoiles (de Banville; Hahn) ki 3481-2 1930?	188740	------	20507		[D;E]
78.	La Delaissée (de Blanchecotte; Hahn) ki 3482-2 1930?	188740	RO 20134	20507		[D;E]
79.	Études latines No. 7: Tyndaris (L. de Lisle; Hahn) ki 3483-2 1930?	188471	------	20508		[D;E]
80.	Études latines No. 5: Lyde (L. de Lisle; Hahn) ki 3484-2 1930?	188471	RO 21034	20508		[D;E]

III. RECORDINGS AS CONDUCTOR

81.* BRUMMELL (1931 opera by Hahn)
Excerpts with the original cast: Jane Morlet, Mlle. Sim-Viva, Louis Arnoult, Lucien Baroux, chorus and orchestra of the Folies Wagram, cond. by Hahn (?) on Odéon 238316, 238317 (ki 4077; ki 4078), and 238318; by M. A. Valsien (?) on Odéon 238321 and 238322. Probably recorded in 1931. [? F]

82.* Ô MON BEL INCONNU (1933 operetta by Hahn)
Collection of vocal excerpts: Pathé PA 36: Ô mon bel inconnu (Huguette Gregory); Qu'est-ce qu'il faut pour être heureux; PA 63: [E204262] Couplets du 2ᵉ acte (Arletty); Chanson à deux voix (Arletty and Hahn); PA 63: [E204265] Air des chapeaux (Ferrant); PA 64: Duo ABC (Gregory and Ferrant); Ô mon bel inconnu (Gregory, Muriel, Morlet)
[Short excerpts w. Hahn: A;B]

83. (Le) Bal de Béatrice d'Este (Ballet suite by Hahn, 1909) French Gramophone Chamber Orchestra, cond. Hahn. (4 12″ sides) Recorded ca. 1936.
(1) Entrée de Ludovic le More (2) Lesquercade [2LA 444-1] L990; Japanese Victor JI 138
(3) Romanesque (4) Ibérienne [2LA 445-1] L990; Japanese Victor JI 138
(5) Léda et l'Oiseau (6) Courante [2LA 446-1] L991; Japanese Victor JI 139
(7) Salut finale au duc de Milan [2LA 447-1] L991; Japanese Victor JI 139

84. Concerto in E Major (Hahn). Magda Tagliafero (pf.) and Orch. cond. Hahn. [6 12″ sides, Pathé PAT-86, PAT-87, PAT-88. No other information.]

85. Concerto No. 26 in D Major (Mozart, K. 537). Magda Tagliatero (pt.) and Pasdeloup Orch. cond. Hahn. [8 12″ sides, Decca TF 141 (fa 126-1/127-2); TF 142 (fa 128-2/129-1); TF 143 (fa 130-1/131-1); TF 144 (fa 132-1/133-1)]

[Following selections "La Voix de son Maître," 10″ Red Label]

86. (Le) MARCHAND DE VENISE: Air de Bassanio "Portia" (Martial Singher) (Hahn)
    OLA 421-1   1935   DA 4871   JE 154

87. (Le) MARCHAND DE VENISE: "L'amour qui" (Heldy, Mahé, Singher, Le Clezio)
    OLA 422-1   1935   DA 4872   JE 155

88. (Le) MARCHAND DE VENISE: Air de Shylock "Je le hais" (André Pernet)
    OLA 423-1   1935   DA 4871   JE 154

89. (Le) MARCHAND DE VENISE: Air de Portia "La sentence nous" (Heldy) (Hahn)
    OLA 424-1   1935   DA 4872   JE 155

IV. RECORDINGS AS SPEAKER

90. Les Instruments de l'orchestre (Ultraphone, four parts, 1935)
    FP 1471:   Part 1 [77596];   Part 2 [77597]
    FP 1472:   Part 3 [77384];   Part 4 [77385]

The following in the French Radio Archives:

91. "Voix célebres" X 682 (31 January 1938).

92. "Faut-il créer en France un théâtre national de l'operette 'Tribune de Paris'?" LO 10599 (no date).

93. Hahn présente "Trois contes de Noël" d'Alphonse Daudet, adaptés par Paul Cas. LO 1021 (12 November 1945).

LONG-PLAYING RECORDS REFERENCED ABOVE

[A]   "The Art of Reynaldo Hahn." SJG Discs [BEV EP 1048 / BEV EP 1049].
[B]   "Reynaldo Hahn." Rococo Records, "Famous Voices of the Past" 5322.
[C]   "Souvenirs of Opera and Song": Seventh Series. IRCC L-7023.
[D]* "Ninon Vallin: Airs d'Opéras et Mélodies." EMI (France) 2910023.
[E]   "Ninon Vallin: La Princesse du Chant." EMI (UK) EX 29 0946 3.
[F]   French Odéon XOC 152 is reported to contain some of the material from Discography No. 81, but this has not been verified.

243

DISCOGRAPHY NOTES

21, 22. No song by this title has been located. It has been suggested that this may have been mis-copied for "L'Hiver" (de Banville; Koechlin), which Hahn is known to have sung.

47. This recording was unpublished until a 1971 special edition was pressed for the British Institute of Recorded Sound "Historic Masters" series.

60. Incorrectly labeled "Les Roses d'Ispahan" on Lp [A].

81. Exactly which sides are conducted by Hahn is not entirely certain.

82. Hahn is named as conductor on both sides of PA 63 and PA 64, but the conductor has not been verified for PA 36. The first side only of PA 63 is included in Lp [A], while only the "Chanson à deux voix" portion (by Arletty and Hahn) is included in Lp [B].

[D] The French Lp Vallin edition lists the earlier recordings of Hahn's "L'Heure exquise" [ki 1618-2] and "Si mes vers avaient des ailes" [ki 1619-2] as originally issued on Odéon 78 rpm 188579 (UK Parlophone RO 20068; US Decca 20504, Australian Parlophone AR 121) as accompanied by Hahn. None of the 78-rpm issues noted ever carried this credit, nor does the UK Lp issue. These two recordings were not made at the same session as Discography Nos. 73–80, which always carried Hahn's name as accompanist on the 78-rpm labels.

ACKNOWLEDGMENTS

My thanks to Harold M. Barnes for permission to use material from his pioneering work on Reynaldo Hahn (written with V. Girard), which is found in the January 1966 issue of *Recorded Sound.* Desmond Shawe-Taylor kindly furnished information on Lp [A] noted above. Special thanks to Alan Kelly for information from his files on the recordings of the Compagnie Française du Gramophone.